The Last Goodbye

Jeremy Bishopp

The Last Goodbye

All Scripture quotations are taken from the
Holy Bible, New International Version® NIV®
Copyright © 1973, 1978, 1984 by International Bible Society
Used by permission. All rights reserved worldwide.

Drawings by Simon Bishopp

Published by Lighthouse Evangelism
Barnstaple. Devon
email: johnchapter3v.16@protonmail.com

ISBN: 9781800491816

Contents

Introduction   page   5

The Wood Mouse   page   9

The Razor   page   12

The Snowman   page   17

Umbrellas   page   21

The Prize   page   25

Blood Donors   page   29

Sheep   page   33

Spring   page   38

The Inferiority Complex   page   43

The Carpenter   page   46

Brambles, Nettles and Other Undesirables   page   50

Rejection   page   54

The Concert   page   58

Niagara Falls   page   62

Twigs   page   67

Swans   page   71

The Christmas Tree   page   76

Candle Smoke   page   80

The Spider's Web   page   84

The Last Goodbye   page   88

Closing Thoughts   page   92

Introduction

As you read this book I want to assure you that it is not about boring religion, deadly dull sermons, and all the robes and rituals which people often associate with church, thinking that's what God and Christianity is all about. It's not about having to live lives which are solemn, even miserable, and with no fun in them,which again some people think is what it's like if you're 'religious'. I have to be honest and say that that's what I used to think it was like, and that image was one of the things that kept me away from God for many years. Instead, this book tells the reality of knowing God, which is totally opposite to everything I've just described, and shows how He brings us happiness, peace, purpose, how He helps us with our problems, and will provide all we need to live fulfilled lives.

Before I became a Christian I had no idea about all that it meant, church wasn't something I'd been brought up with, I'd never read the Bible, and it was all completely new to me. I had heard about the life and death of Jesus when I was 16, but it was over 17 years later that I finally came to God, with very little understanding of it all. I realise that as you read this book you may well be in the same position as I was, and so at this stage some of the things in the stories might be hard to understand, or may not make sense. Because of that, I just want to give a brief explanation now of the situations we can find ourselves in, who Jesus is, why He came to earth, and the difference He can make in our lives. Then the truth of what I've written should be clear, and understandable.

You see, so many people are looking for peace, hope, security, help, direction, and so much more, but don't really know where to look. It doesn't matter where people search, or what they try, they never find the answers, their lives are never fulfilled, and there is always something missing. Add to that the fact that these days it's often so difficult to know who you can trust, and who you can believe, whether it's in those in public life, or in individual relationships, and the scale of the difficulties and struggles becomes clearer.

The problem is, every human being leads a life which is a long way from being perfect. Whether we are rich or poor, famous or unknown, whatever race or colour we are, we all have similar hopes, fears, joys, and sorrows There are also things we do, think, and say, which we know are wrong, which are called sins. Those sins may be large or small, out in the open, or hidden away, but they have a huge effect. On a world scale they are the cause of wars, torture, persecution, poverty, and so much more. On a personal level those wrong things, those sins, can be equally destructive.

However we may try to justify ourselves, sins lead to guilt, they take away our peace, they cause relationship problems, and so much more, and most important of all, they separate us from God. Why is that important? Because God will judge us for what we have done, but He also loves each one of us so much, whoever we are, and whatever we have done, that He wants to help us and bless us, and He can sort out our problems. We may know about Him, we may sometimes even pray to Him, but God is holy, that is, without sin, and our sin creates a barrier between Him and us.

Imagine standing outside the gates of Buckingham Palace, wanting to go in and meet a member of the royal family, but you've no invitation, so you have to stay outside the gates. Even though you know that person is in the palace, the barrier keeps you apart, and keeps you from having any relationship with them. That's like the barrier between us and God, which keeps us from really knowing Him, and allowing Him to help us, but there's an answer to it. The good news is that God offers a free invitation to meet Him to everyone who wants it. So how does He do that? Let me explain.

The birth and death of Jesus Christ, and other things about Him were prophesied, that is, told about Him, hundreds of times in the Bible, written as much as 1,700 years before His birth, all of which He fulfilled. There is more historical evidence to prove that Jesus lived than there is for Julius Caesar landing in Britain. There is no doubt that Jesus lived, and that He was crucified by the Romans. More than that though, the Bible says He is the Son of God, that He was God come to earth in human form. Jesus Himself said that He is the Son of God, and that He came to take the sins of the world on Himself. Quite simply, He was saying that He would pay the price for us for all the things we've done wrong, so that God would forgive us. How did He achieve that? Well, Jesus came to earth, born in a stable in Bethlehem, He grew into a man, and then, when He was 33 years old He died, crucified on a cross, even though He was totally innocent. That death is what He came for, the death He knew He was going to have, and as He died He was taking the punishment that we deserve on Himself. He was paying the price for the sins of the world, and that means yours and mine.

After He had been killed His body was laid in a tomb, and that's where He stayed, until three days later, in fulfilment of what was prophesied hundreds of years before, and as Jesus had said would happen, God brought Him back to life, and many people saw Him alive again. This is not fantasy, it's an historical fact, witnessed by many people. In so doing, Jesus defeated death and sin, never to die again, and was then taken up to heaven, where He lives forever.

Seems far fetched? Well, not really. There are confirmed cases of God raising people from the dead over many centuries, even up to the present day, and for God who created this whole universe, including us, to raise Jesus from the dead was quite a simple thing. It was the price Jesus had to pay in the first place that was so very costly, and so hard for Him to have to do. Also, the proof that all this happened is shown by the fact that Jesus only spent three years in Israel telling people about the way to find God before He was killed, He only had twelve disciples (that is close followers), and yet belief in Him has gone all round the world. Christianity is by far the largest faith in the world, and that is only because He has shown over nearly 2,000 years that He is still alive, and is the Son of God.

God knew our problems, and that we can never be good enough for Him in our own strength, and He knew that the only way to help us was to have someone to pay the price for those things we've done wrong. That someone was Jesus, and because He is the Son of

God, He is the only one who has ever lived a perfect life with no sin, because God's power was in Him to enable Him to do that. We can never be perfect, so God sent Jesus to be the perfect sacrifice for us, to die for our sins in our place. He paid the price for you and me. That sacrifice was made once only, it never needs to be repeated, and it is an everlasting sacrifice which applies in our lives today, just as much as it did nearly 2,000 years ago when He made it. Sounds strange? It's true, and everything you have just read is explained in much greater detail in the Bible, along with reports of the miracles Jesus and His followers did through the mighty power of God.

Jesus is love, and even if we don't realise it, He loves each one of us so much more than we can ever know. Because Jesus took all our sins on Himself, and because He is alive for evermore, He is called the Saviour of the world, but to have our sins forgiven we have to accept Him as our own personal Saviour. Now, for many people, that's where it starts to get difficult, or even to seem impossible. To be forgiven, and to be put right with God, means we have to open ourselves up to Jesus, and that can seem a very hard, even a scary thing to do. I know, because I was like that, but that's not what the reality of Jesus is like. He is love, total and utter love.

Being the Son of God He is able, when we are willing to let Him, to come into our lives through His Spirit, to forgive us for all our sins, to give us the peace or help we are desperate for, and give us a fresh start. What do we have to do to earn that? Absolutely nothing! Forgiveness, peace, and release from the past are free gifts from God, with the compliments of Jesus, because He has already paid the price for us. That's where our free invitation to meet with God comes from. All we have to do is ask, and that costs us nothing, except perhaps surrendering our own pride, and maybe even our stubbornness, and recognising that it's what we need, and what we want Him to do for us.

Let me encourage you as you read these stories,which are totally true, to ignore whatever images of religion there may be around, and instead see the reality of the great love God has for you.

The Wood Mouse

One of my favourite pastimes is to walk through the local woods. It's a very simple pleasure, but for me one of the most beautiful places to go to is an English wood. The variety of birds singing, the diversity of the trees, not just in their different species, but in such varied shapes as well, spring flowers, autumn leaves, toadstools, chestnuts, and so much more, all serve to make the woods a wonderful place at any time of year. Add to that the opportunity at times to watch foxes, and even deer, and you have a view of just a small part of the incredible beauty and order of God's creation.

One morning as I was walking along a pathway I had travelled many times before, I suddenly heard a rustling near my feet. Stopping, I looked down, and there, moving slowly through the leaves and ivy was a wood mouse, the smallest of our native mice. I would have expected it to run away when it saw me, but it didn't. It wasn't that in me it recognised a modern day Francis of Assisi, and so decided to stay and enjoy me talking to it. The reason it didn't run was that stuck to one of its back feet was a snail. To me that snail was tiny, and I could have carried it so easily, without it slowing me down at all, but to the mouse it was obviously a big problem. How it came to be stuck on the mouse's foot I have no idea, but the snail was in its shell, and the normally wet sticky base had dried hard like glue.

I picked up two twigs, and was able to gently hold the mouse down with one, whilst trying to prise the snail off with the other, but it was stuck fast. I didn't have gloves with me, and so I wasn't willing to pick it up and risk being infected if the mouse had bitten or scratched me. Even if I'd had them I was too far from home to take the mouse back and soak its foot until the snail came off. The only thing I could have done would have been to use force with the twigs to pull the snail away, but in doing so I may well have pulled its leg off, and so I had no choice but to let it go, carrying the burden with it, hoping that the next time it rained the water would wash it free.

It disappeared into the undergrowth, but whether it survived or not I don't know.

However, as I thought about this incident later, I realised that this is such a good illustration of our lives. We start off free from care, but then we start doing things that we know are wrong, that we shouldn't do, and which are known as sins. Gradually more and more sins creep, and sometimes gallop in, and as we go through life the load gets harder and harder to bear. Just like the wood mouse, we are burdened down with things which shouldn't be there, which are clinging on fast, and which we can't get free from, no matter how hard we try. As humans we can try pushing them into the background, but deep down they are still there, bringing us down, and preventing us from living the life God wants us to live. That mouse was unable to live the life it was meant to, because it was carrying a burden it wasn't designed to carry. So it is with us. Sins, whether big or small, take away our joy, our happiness, our peace, our hope. The memories and the consequences linger on, and place on us a burden we weren't designed to carry.

Compared to that mouse my power is immense, but the only way I could have helped it right where it was would have been to force the snail off, damaging the mouse, and leaving it maimed or dying. I didn't have at my disposal what was needed to set it free, and so I let it go, carrying its burden with it. In contrast, God has power which is truly immense, no matter what you compare that power to, and He wants to use it in our lives in a way that is so loving and gentle, if only we will let Him. The mouse had no choice but to let me try to help it, but God gives us the choice of whether we want to accept His help, or reject it - He never forces His way in. I don't know how the mouse had become stuck, but I wanted to set it free. God knows everything about every one of us, including all the wrong things we've done, and He doesn't just want to take one burden off us, He wants to set us totally free, to wash all of the past clean and give us a new start, and real hope for the future. So how does He do it? It begins simply by us asking Jesus to forgive us, to be in our lives, and to bring us into the relationship with God which then opens the way for Him to help us.

At best, I would have severely damaged that mouse, but God will never damage anyone when they come to Him and ask for His help. On the contrary, the damage was done to Jesus, when ordinary men flogged Him and crucified Him, so that we may be set free through the love and grace of God. If I'd had water available I would have been able to free the mouse. The forgiveness won for sinful human beings through the blood Jesus shed on that cross has been available ever since that event, and it's available for you now. He sacrificed His blood to pay the price for your sins and mine.

When we come to God the Father through His Son Jesus Christ, all our burdens can be removed, and we can be set free painlessly, even though we don't deserve to be. The mouse had no choice but to carry on dragging its burden around, but we have the choice to continue carrying our burdens, or to let God take them off us, and to make us free indeed. All we have to do is ask.

The Razor

These days there are so many amazing pieces of technology we can have in our homes. From the television to the DVD player, the computer, the dishwasher, the cordless 'phone, and so much more, the list we can have to make our lives easier, and, supposedly, better, just goes on and on. One modern invention I really appreciate may not seem that special, it's certainly not packed full of sophisticated devices, and a lot of people may not think much of it, but for me it's great. It's the electric razor.

Now that may not seem much to enthuse over, but mine is a real blessing to me. Why? Because over the years it has saved me losing so much blood, and saved me so much time trying to stop cuts bleeding. For some reason I can't explain, I find it almost impossible to use an ordinary wet razor without cutting myself. It may be just a small nick, or even several, or it may be a bigger cut needing more effort to stop the blood, but however careful I am, it still happens. On the very rare occasions I've managed to shave without cutting myself, it's almost a reason to put the flags out, or for the national papers to cover the story.

It's always been a nuisance having to sort out the cuts, but on one occasion it was particularly embarrassing. Many years ago now I was elected in the local elections as a district councillor for our village. A few days later all the councillors of the party I stood for had to attend an introductory morning meeting at the council offices. Because it was my first time there, and I didn't want to be late, I was hurrying to ensure I was ready in plenty of time. Wet shaves and me don't go together when I'm being careful. A wet shave when I'm in a hurry is a recipe for disaster, and that morning, shaving above my top lip I managed to slice into myself very easily and painfully. The blood flowed, and in spite of all my efforts to staunch it, I was still bleeding when I left home, still bleeding when I reached the council offices, and still bleeding during the meeting. Finally, after constant pressing with my handkerchief the bleeding stopped.

I'm sure no-one else at that meeting would have any memory of it now, but I can still remember how awkward I felt, and how I was so pleased when it did finally stop. I explained to some people what had happened, but I still felt embarrassed. If I'd been using an electric razor it wouldn't have happened, and I would have had a far more comfortable first meeting.

There can be problems with electric razors though, and one of the most obvious ones is if there is no power. They will of course only work if there is a source of electricity to plug them into. Even mine, which can be used from the mains, or from the built in rechargeable battery, will only last on the battery for a limited time unless it is plugged in to the power again. Also, an electric razor can't help you the way it could if you are in Toronto and the razor is still in Heathrow. That's what happened with my luggage some years ago, and the only option then was to buy some cheap wet razors at the airport to use until mine was re-united with me some 24 hours, and more cuts later.

So how does an electric razor relate to having God in my life?

Well, first of all, for many years, in spite of the problems, I had kept away from electric razors because I didn't think they were very good. The only one I had tried hadn't shaved me as well as my wet one, so I kept to what I knew. The cuts kept coming, the blood kept coming, and I hated shaving, but I put up with it because the alternative didn't seem to offer me anything. Finally I tried another electric razor, the results were very good, there was no blood, and from that moment I was totally sold on them, and I've never wanted to go back to what I had before.

Many people are like that about Christianity, and I was too. They know they aren't happy with their lives, whilst some are extremely unhappy, and others even hate the life they are living, but it's all they know, and they feel safer staying where they are than giving God a try. They may have tried going to church, as I did once, and found it totally irrelevant and boring, and decided not to try it again. They may have been put off God by the image that comes across from too many church leaders with prominent profiles in the media, who seem to have little faith, and nothing to offer anyone. I was, and it can keep us away from God without giving Him a chance to show what He is really like, and what He can do to help us. It wasn't until I found a good razor that I realised the benefits, and it wasn't until I decided to let go of the past, and allow God to come into my life that I began to realise the enormous benefits He gives to us.

My first, one off experience of a church was a bad one, but later I was unexpectedly invited to another church, and reluctantly went. To my surprise it was good, and had an excellent minister who had real faith. I understood what he was saying about the love Jesus has for us, I became a Christian, and I was sold on this new life. Just as I never want to go back to a wet razor, I never want to go back to my old life, because it has nothing to offer me that is worthwhile.

The problem with Christianity is that it only works when we stay connected to God, and allow Him to be the motivating force in our lives. Just as an electric razor looks good, but only works when it is connected to the power, many people may seem to give a good appearance by going to church, but in actual fact they have no real relationship with God, they are not true followers of Jesus in the way He wants them to be, and consequently they are not connected up to the life changing power of God, and it shows. Unfortunately, sometimes others will judge God by the impression some of those people who are like that can give. Yes, they go to church, even though the reality of God doesn't affect them, but when they do things wrong people will think that's what all Christians are like, and consequently that God is like that too, which isn't the case at all.

In contrast, true Christians know the power of God in their lives. Like everyone else, they aren't perfect, they will still make mistakes, and get things wrong, but they are willing to apologise, and ask for forgiveness. They are willing to let God change and bless them, and to help them to bless other people too, and they stay connected.

When I was in Toronto, I knew my razor existed, but I could make no connection with it some 3,000 miles away in Heathrow, and so it couldn't help me the way it was normally able to, and the way I wanted it to. For many people, God seems to be not just 3,000 miles away, but a million miles away, and yet the reality is that He is as close as we want Him to be. I knew I owned a good razor, but if I'd deliberately chosen to do without it, and leave it at home, I couldn't have blamed anyone else once I started cutting myself again with a wet one. Sadly, so many people deliberately choose to leave God behind wherever they go, but so often, as soon as something goes wrong, even when it's their fault, God gets the blame.

Many people have the wrong image of God, and think that He's an ogre, or a kill joy, maybe even that He's cruel and wants to mess up our lives. Some think God should intervene in every bad situation that happens in the world, but if He then intervened in something they were doing wrong that would be different, and they wouldn't want Him to do that. The reality is that God is not like that at all, and the reason bad things happen is because He gives us all free will to do what we want, even to reject Him if we choose to. The trouble is, when people do that they are missing out on the truth of what God is really like. Just as I was originally with the razor, and my initial thoughts about Christianity, they don't see how much God loves them, and the great blessings He can give.

A razor is designed to help the person who chooses to use it. God delights to help people who choose to come to Him, and ask Him for help. I could do nothing to get my razor until it was flown over in my luggage the next day. Anyone can find God whenever they choose to find Him. He's not a million miles away, He's just a prayer away, and the only delay we have in finding Him is the delay we impose on ourselves when we refuse to really reach out to Him, and allow Him into our lives.

The Snowman

One Christmas, some years ago now, we went to stay with my brother and his family in Northern Ireland. It's always good to get together, and, even before Christmas Day arrived, we were having a great time, not doing anything special, just enjoying each other's company. On Christmas morning my wife and I woke early (it wasn't the excitement of expecting Father Christmas to have been, as he doesn't come any more!), and, as we looked out of the window, we saw that everywhere was white with snow. It was a lovely start to a special day.

After breakfast we went to the service at the church where my brother was the pastor, and there we focused on the reality of what Christmas is all about. For many outside, as it is everywhere, Jesus was obviously not a priority, as a jogger ran by, and cars regularly went past the building, but for us, focusing on the love God has for everyone, shown in the birth of His Son, was the most important thing. Then it was back home to open the presents, given as an expression of our love for each other, and after that it was time to enjoy our Christmas lunch.

In the afternoon, my niece wanted to build a snowman, so, with my wife, we agreed to help her, as any dutiful uncle and aunt should. I would like to be able to give the excuse that my niece was a little girl, so obviously we needed to help her, but I can't. In the summer of that year, at the age of 22, she had graduated from university, and now, like three big kids, we were in the garden, having a great time, doing something I hadn't done for many years. My only excuse is that I was given the wrong name at birth, as I should really have been called Peter Pan. I still get pleasure in simple things like that, just as I did as a child, and even now I refuse to be totally grown up. Still, Jesus did say that we have to change and become like little children to enter the kingdom of heaven, so I guess my childlike attitude is alright - God does want us to have innocent fun, and enjoy our lives, and to trust Him with our cares and burdens, as a child can with its parents.

Soon my brother joined us, showing his humility as a church minister in being willing to help his childish flock in their task, and before long the snowman was finished. Then the inevitable snowball fight ensued. It was great, with my brother and myself being the last to finish 'playing'. Finally it was time for us to go in, very satisfied with what we had done, and the pleasure it had given us.

There had been a problem though with the snowman as we were building it. Before the snow came the ground had been very wet from the rain, and as we rolled the snow across the grass to make it into very large balls, it was also collecting a layer of mud on every turn. Undeterred, we had carried on, until we had ended up with the rough, though muddy shape of a snowman, nearly six feet high. It couldn't be left like that, so we had carefully collected handfuls of clean snow to put on as the outer coating, and, after quite a lot of effort, it at last stood there, white, and looking like a snowman. Coal was added for the eyes, and a carrot for the nose, and it was ready to be admired.

For some reason which I don't understand, I expected that, when it melted, all the mud would be washed down, leaving the gradually diminishing snowman still looking white. Unfortunately I was wrong. The next day it was raining, and it wasn't long before the coating disappeared, leaving the muddy base exposed. Over the next two days, the mud seemed to be the dominant feature, and there was nothing attractive about our snowman any more, which was a shame. It didn't really matter though - we had had pleasure building it, and given ourselves happy memories to look back on, and it was only snow. However, every human being can be like that snowman, and that really matters, because every human being matters.

Just like the snowman, we can have layers and layers of dirt in our lives. Oh, they can be hidden under that false covering we may put on for the benefit of others, but they are still there. Very few people will win an Oscar for acting, but every human being is a great actor, and many could win an Oscar for the role they play everyday. The things we are ashamed of, the things we wish we had or hadn't done, the years of carrying guilt, are all safely covered up by the mask we put on, and become so accustomed to wearing. We hope that people will see us the way we would like them to see us, the person we would like to be, not the real, flawed person, which, like everyone else on this planet, we know we are. The problem is, that it makes no difference how well we play the role, God sees the reality beneath the mask all day, everyday. We can't cover up what we have done, or what we are, hoping that He will not realise the truth about us.

For us, as the snowman melted, there was nothing we could do to redeem the situation, it was becoming an unsightly mess. There was no fresh snow to make it look good again, and we had to give up on it. Contrast that with what God can do in even the ugliest, the dirtiest, the vilest of lives. Through the blood of Jesus He can wash away every layer of dirt, every single sin a person has ever committed. Why? Because, as I've said, unlike the snowman, which wasn't a real person, and didn't matter, people's lives are real, and what they do, and what they become, matters so much to God, and He never gives up on us. No-one is beyond His forgiveness and restoration. His love for every human being is so overwhelming that

He was willing to send Jesus to die for each one of us.

If we had been able to build our snowman with clean snow all the way through, even as it melted it would still have looked good, and we would still have been pleased with it. When we come to Jesus, and allow Him to forgive our sins, and wash us clean right through, the promise in the Bible which says, "Even though your sins are like scarlet, they shall be as white as snow", is fulfilled. That is how John Newton, who was a slave trader, a fornicator, and a vile man, was totally changed.

For years he had been completely against God, wanting nothing to do with Him, but during a fierce storm, which nearly destroyed the ship he was on, he recognised his need for forgiveness, and cried out to Jesus to help him. There, in the midst of extreme danger, he was forgiven, and miraculously, the ship finally managed to reach Ireland safely. Jesus washed those scarlet sins clean, John Newton turned from his evil ways, and was able to write the words, in the hymn which is known around the world, 'Amazing grace, how sweet the sound, that saved a wretch like me'. Because of Jesus, God saw John Newton as perfect, whiter than snow, and that grace is still available today for all who come to Him.

Umbrellas

I really like umbrellas. To me there is something very special about being out in the rain, especially if I don't have a coat on to protect me, and having an umbrella keeping me dry. The large golf type I have now is much more effective at covering me than the smaller ones I used to use, and to be out in a downpour with it and not get wet is a thing I really like. Okay, it may sound strange, but I think it goes back to childhood days, when there were times of finding shelter from the rain, and the excitement it would bring in having something to cover and protect me from the elements. Even now, sheltering under a tree with dense foliage still affects me, and brings out the child in me again, so it's not just umbrellas that do it to me. Obviously though, it is more convenient to carry an umbrella around with me than a tree, and, when necessary, I can take it with me wherever I go to give me instant cover.

However there can be a few problems with umbrellas which make them much less effective than they need to be. I suppose the most obvious one is that they can blow inside out, and so when the wind is strong, and you really need that protection, you can't risk using it. I know a lot of modern ones can be turned the right way out again, but, whilst you are struggling to do that, you can still get very wet. With the older ones, when that happens they are no more use, and have to be thrown away. They can of course wear out, or, what can happen before then, is that they are lost, often by leaving them on a bus or train. I once did that, and, because mine had been a present and I valued it, I took the trouble to go to the lost property office at Waterloo Station. Mine had a slight tear in the leather covering on the handle, and, amazingly, because of that I was able to find it amongst literally hundreds of others. It appeared though that most of those in the racks would never be reclaimed, and so they would no longer give their owners the protection they once had. That covering would be transferred to someone else when they were sold off, and the original owner would have to buy a new one.

Another problem, even with the golf umbrellas, is that they are not large enough to cover two people totally. On a number of occasions I have tried to keep my wife or my mother dry, as well as myself, when we have only had one umbrella between us, but it's never very effective, because there just isn't room for two people to get completely under it.

One more thing is that horses are afraid of umbrellas. I don't know why, but they really are. I guess that's why you never see a horse carrying an umbrella! Being serious, they are frightened by them. One morning I was walking past a field, using the umbrella, and I stopped to look at three horses grazing. They spotted me, and as I stood there they became more and more unsettled. They started circling round, gradually moving further away from me, then they stopped, before starting to circle and move away again. Now when I'm using an umbrella, whenever I see a horse and rider coming towards me I always put it down, and the rider always thanks me, because they know how it would scare the horse if I didn't.

Let me now compare, but contrast these difficulties with God's love. In the Bible there is a line which says 'His banner over me is love', and that banner, that covering, is available to everyone who wants it, and it is complete. As I said, an umbrella can blow inside out when the wind is too strong, but absolutely nothing is too strong for God to handle, nothing is too difficult for Him. In the midst of our storms, our struggles, our trials, one thing is constant - the love of God which says, "Never will I leave you; never will I forsake you". Whatever problems we are labouring with, the covering of the love of God can bring rest to our souls, and bring us safely through the storm.

Umbrellas may wear out, but the love of God never has and never will. The love of God never ceases, and He is always there, wanting to look after us, to help us, and to bless us. God never loses His love for each one of us, even when we choose to reject Him, and He never loses sight of us. He loves us in spite of what we are or what we do, and He chooses to forgive and cover us through the blood of Jesus when we ask Him to.

I searched for my umbrella, because I really wanted to find it, and didn't want to lose it, but for a long time, just like those umbrellas which nobody looked for, I didn't look for God. At last, after years of keeping Him at bay, I finally realised how important it was to have His forgiveness. I then searched for God, because I really wanted to find Him. I didn't need the boring, irrelevant religion I talked about previously, but I knew I needed God, and that's totally different. I didn't want to lose the gift of eternal life Jesus offered me, and I have never regretted it - it truly was the best thing I ever did. Sadly, to so many people, finding God is no more important than finding an umbrella at the lost property office, and they choose to leave Him on the shelf. For them He is just as irrelevant, just as insignificant, and yet God promises that when we search for Him we will find Him, because He wants us to, and He wants us to come under the covering of His love, so that He can bless us.

His love is sufficient for everybody. He doesn't have to give each of us just a small part, so that we are partially covered, and all have to huddle up together to try to be covered by as much as possible. He gives all of us all His love when we want to receive it. No-one is ever rejected when they ask, no-one is given short measure, and He will not take His love away. In the Bible, a man called Paul, a follower of Jesus, wrote "For I am convinced that neither death nor life, nor angels nor demons, neither the present nor the future, nor any powers, neither height nor depth, nor anything else in all creation, will be able to separate us from the love of God that is in Christ Jesus our Lord".

Finally, just like the horses, so many people are afraid of God's love even though there is nothing to fear. I can understand that, because, as well as being put off by what I thought was boring, irrelevant religion, as I said in The Razor story, for years, before I became a Christian, I'd thought I would have to change almost instantly. I thought I would suddenly have to become so 'holy', and such a completely different person overnight that I couldn't handle it, and I didn't want that. In all honesty though, nobody could cope with a complete, instant personality transformation, and God knows that. The trouble was that I didn't realise God knew it. I knew I should have God in my life, but fear is what kept Him at bay.

Looking back now, having been a Christian for many years, I realise how misguided my thinking was. After all, God designed us, He made us, He knows what makes us tick, He knows everything about us, and He knows the best way to help us, so He would hardly do something to completely mess us up. I hadn't realised that when I eventually came to the point when I let the fear go, and allowed Him into my life, He would come in such a gentle and loving way that I could see that in the love of God there is absolutely nothing to fear. Gradually, gently, lovingly, over the years He has been changing me in ways I am very happy with, and I still want more. Perfect love drives away all fear, and God is total and perfect love.

The Prize

Some years ago, my mother had some really good news. She had an official notification in the post telling her that she had won a lot of money. In the top left hand corner of the letter it said, in large bold print, 'YOU HAVE DONE IT, MRS BISHOPP! Underneath, again in bold, though this time slightly smaller print, it proclaimed, 'OFFICIAL ANNOUNCEMENT:' (underlined to show that it was definitely official), and then below that in normal sized print, 'Mrs Bishopp, WINNER, RECEIVES'. Below that in the large bold print again '£20,000'. Finally, highlighted in a box, was her registered claim number, with the statement, 'GRAND PRIZE PENDING'. She had obviously won, or so it seemed.

At the top of the page, from the middle, going across to the edge, in very small capital letters it also said, 'Please follow the instructions! If you return the winning registered claim number in our draw by midnight one week from Tuesday - as required - we will be able to declare for the record'. It seemed a strange sentence to have there in that position, but that's what was going to happen. All she had to do was return the form in time, and the money was hers. Below that, this time in red, and in larger capitals it said, 'Sign the back of this notice, return the winning entry form and the £20,000.00 cheque is definitely yours!' The letter then went on to explain that two other winners had already received their cheques, and that she was in danger of losing her prize if she didn't act quickly.

Now, although the letter had come from a company she had never heard of, it did appear genuine. They did sell extremely expensive chocolates which she would never normally be tempted to buy, and on the back of the letter one of the conditions was that she had to send back the enclosed order form, making her choices from the catalogue of the products which appealed to her the most. The form had to be returned, as that also had the registered claim number printed on it. It did say that no purchase was necessary, but surely that defeated the object of the exercise for them, so it would be sensible to keep them happy by giving an order, the cost of course being only a fraction of the value of the prize.

As it seemed too good to be true, my mother asked me to look at the letter. I read it through, but it did appear that she had won, although it didn't make sense. I read it again, convinced there had to be a catch, but I still couldn't see it. I didn't understand why the sentence in tiny print was where it was at the top of the page, but that was all. Finally, I decided to go through it all in minute detail, and then I found it. One tiny dot made all the difference. The strange sentence didn't end with the words, 'for the record'. Instead of being a full stop, it was in fact a colon, and suddenly everything became clear. It had all been so deviously laid out that the 'OFFICIAL ANNOUNCEMENT' line didn't follow the opening sentence at all, but instead followed the word 'record'. My mother would only win the prize if hers was the winning claim number picked out from no doubt many thousands who had received the same letter. Needless to say, she didn't return the form, but many may well have been tricked.

Unfortunately, these days it seems that so many companies resort to using wording which is not all that it appears to say, and so often there is a get out clause, ensuring they make as much money as possible. It may seem surprising, but even in the Bible God has put what we could call a get out clause. We can find it in what is known as the Old Testament, in chapter 53 of the book written by a man called Isaiah, who was a prophet. He wrote accurately, 700 years before it happened, 'He was pierced for our transgressions, He was crushed for our iniquities, the punishment that brought us peace was upon Him, and by His wounds we are healed." He wrote that about Jesus, knowing He would be flogged almost beyond human recognition, that His hands and feet would be pierced as He was nailed to a cross, that His side would be pierced with a spear, and that He would die for us.

God then confirmed it, as recorded in the New Testament, in each of what are known as the four Gospels, when we read just how and why Jesus was crucified for us, taking the punishment for our sins upon Himself, so that all of us can be forgiven and have peace. That was what God wrote, and then put into action, in the get out clause that was solely to benefit each of us, and not, like modern companies, to benefit them at our expense.

It's the get out clause which says that no matter how much turmoil you may be in, come to the Son, and He will give you peace. It's the get out clause which says, 'I know your every need, and if you will only come to Me I will meet those needs'. It's the get out clause which says you can get free from depression, feeling hopeless, free from hurts, loneliness, or adultery. You can be free from alcoholism, drug addiction, gambling addiction, or whatever else you may be struggling with, if you will let Jesus, the Son of God set you free. It's the get out clause which says you can get out of having to go to hell when you die, and instead you can have perfect peace with God forever as a free gift.

It's the get out clause which says, 'I don't want your money, or your possessions, the whole world belongs to me anyway. All I want from you is your love, and your trust, and for you to follow Jesus, allowing Him to be your Saviour and your guide. In return, I will give you more blessings, and more help than you could ever dream of. Your life will be fulfilled, and really worth living, if only you will come to Me through following My Son'. It's the get out clause which says all this is a free gift because I love you so much.

On a number of occasions I had the thrill of discovering that, like many others, I had reached the final round of the prize draw of a famous, and now extinct, monthly publication. The six potentially valuable prize numbers went back in the envelope with 'No' on it, rejecting the latest book offer, and I waited, with not such baited breath, for the cheque to arrive. It never did.

Every week, millions of people spend millions of pounds buying lottery tickets, hoping that this week it could be them, and every week, for millions of people, it isn't. I once knew a pensioner who was spending about £1,000 a year on tickets, and every week he was disappointed. Contrast that with what God offers. With Him it is not a lottery, with just one, or maybe a few winners every week getting the prize He is giving away. The gift is there for everyone who wants it, and who responds by asking to receive it. It's no good just believing that Jesus lived, and then going no further than that. Like any gift, it will only make a difference if we have it in our life.

For everyone who is willing to take a step of faith, to accept the fact that Jesus died on the cross for them, and then to follow Him, God promises that He will never turn them away, and will accept them totally. It is summed up so well in what is probably the most famous verse in the Bible, in what is known as John's Gospel - 'For God so loved the world that He gave His one and only Son, that whoever believes in Him shall not perish but have eternal life' (John 3 verse16). Now that's what you call a get out clause!

Blood Donors

I was working with a friend of mine one day, and, as we neared the end of what we were doing, he opened the garage door for us to put the tools inside. It was the lift up type, and unfortunately didn't go up as high as it should have done. He warned me to be careful, as nearly half of it was still sticking out at an angle, the warning was duly noted, and we continued collecting the tools. However, by the time I approached the garage again my thoughts were elsewhere, and somehow I didn't see the danger, with the result that the corner of the door suddenly gouged into the top of my head. It was very painful for a few minutes, and it took some time to stop bleeding, but that was all. Contrast that with Jesus, when, before His crucifixion, the Roman soldiers pushed a crown of thorns firmly into His head. It must have been agony, but there was no relief from it, the thorns stayed. I knew the danger, and forgot about it, but, unlike me, Jesus knew the danger, and deliberately chose to accept it - He had been born specifically to be crucified for our sins.

A couple of weeks earlier I had been to give blood, something I had done many times before without any problems, but this time the woman who put the needle in my arm did an awful job. It was very painful as she did it, and even as I was lying on the bed as the blood was being taken, it was still uncomfortable, and afterwards resulted in me having a bruise about two inches across. I would never normally complain, but afterwards I 'phoned the Blood Transfusion service, partly to say what happened, as she needed more training, as usually there is very little discomfort in giving blood, but mainly because I didn't want her putting other people off for the future.

Unlike me, Jesus didn't just have a bit of pain, and a 2 inch bruise to complain about. With the crown of thorns in place, the soldiers then struck him on the head again and again with a staff, they hit Him in the face, and they flogged Him mercilessly, ripping open His flesh, and yet He made no complaint. Ater all this He didn't have a small, sharp needle inserted in an artery. Instead, heavy iron nails were cruelly hammered through His hands and feet into the cross. He was taking the agonising punishment that we deserved, and that is what He was born for.

Before giving blood, a sample drop is taken from the finger, and then put into a bottle containing green or blue liquid. If the donor is anaemic it will float, but if the blood is of a good enough quality it will sink, and then the donation can be given. Later, that donated blood will be thoroughly tested to ensure it is safe to give to a patient. For the blood of Jesus to be of a high enough quality to prove Him to be the only Saviour of the world, His life had to fulfil the hundreds of prophecies written about Him over many centuries before His birth. He had to be born in the family line of King David, Israel's most famous king, He had to be born to a virgin, and in the town of Bethlehem, He had to be beaten beyond recognition, to be crucified with criminals, and to be buried in a rich man's tomb, to name just a few. Whatever the prophecy, He fulfilled it, He passed the test, and He was counted worthy to shed His blood for the sins of us all.

Over the centuries many have claimed to have been sent by God with special teaching to lead a group of followers, or even that they were a god themselves, but none of them fulfilled any of the prophecies that the true Saviour had to fulfil. Only Jesus was able to do that. Some people say that what is written about the life and death of Jesus was made to fit in with the prophecies, but if Jesus is just a dead, false prophet, there is one prophecy that neither He, nor the followers He had, could do anything about after He had died.

In the Bible, Isaiah, writing, as I've previously mentioned, about the Saviour, or Messiah as He is also known, and some 700 years before Jesus was born, said that, after His death, '"The will of the Lord will prosper in His hand." No dead, false saviour could make that happen, and yet that is what has been happening for nearly 2,000 years. Still today, and every day, many millions throughout the world are finding the way to God through Jesus Christ. They are finding that everything written about Jesus in the Bible is true. Still today He brings new life, He brings peace, He sets people free from whatever binds them, and so much more. The will of the Lord is still prospering in His hand, He is the Saviour, His blood has passed every test.

Even when my blood has been found to be healthy, for many people it is of absolutely no use. Because of the different blood groups, when I give blood it is only of use to those in the same group. Give it to someone else and they will die. If that had been the case with the blood of Jesus we would all have been in trouble. If His blood was to be shed only for those who proved themselves worthy of receiving His forgiveness and love, nobody who has ever lived could qualify. With the exception of Jesus, everyone who has ever lived has sinned, and is not worthy to receive anything from God, and yet Jesus died for us all. In the New Testament, in the book called Romans it says, 'For all have sinned and fall short of the glory of God, and are justified freely by His grace through the redemption' (forgiven and saved from our sin) 'that came by Jesus Christ. God presented Him as a sacrifice of atonement' (paying the price for our sin) 'through faith in His blood'. The price Jesus paid through shedding His blood was not paid for one group only. It was paid for everyone, no matter what their age, colour, nationality, belief, or sins. The blood transfusion Jesus offers is available to all who ask Him for it.

When I have given my blood, and it is kept for someone in the same group, it has to be used within a certain time, as blood has a very limited shelf life. There are not gallons of blood stored up with 'best before' dates on the bottles for 12 or 18 months ahead. The blood cannot be packed full of preservatives like so much of our food, and then kept almost indefinitely. It has to be used within 6 weeks, and if it isn't it has to be disposed of. If that applied to the blood of Jesus, again, we would all be in real trouble. If, only 6 weeks after the crucifixion, it had been found that His blood had passed the sell by date, was of no more use for anyone, and that no-one else could be saved by it, then in reality His sacrifice would have been virtually useless, and meaningless. Then the prophecy from Isaiah would certainly not have been fulfilled. The amazing thing about the blood of Jesus is that throughout all the centuries, it has never lost its power to bring transformation to people's lives. Through His shed blood Jesus still brings forgiveness, and real life, a life that's really worth living, just as He has been doing since He walked this earth.

Finally, when I give blood, it is given with the intention of helping someone I have never met. I don't know what help my blood has been over the years, and to be honest I don't really want or need to know. What I would be very unhappy about though, is if I found out that someone who was critically ill was offered a life saving transfusion of my blood, but they decided to refuse it and died, and the blood I had given was wasted and thrown away. Most people would agree that anyone who refused such an opportunity would be very foolish to have thrown away the offer of life. Sadly, for millions around the world, that is just what they do with the blood of Jesus when they choose not to know Him, even though they could have new life.

Without accepting that sacrifice there is no new life, and instead of an eternal life of joy and peace with God, there is instead eternal torment, literally in hell. It is a terrifying prospect, and yet so many willingly refuse the transfusion. How Jesus feels about it I don't know, but I'm sure it must be far more than just sadness. If my blood had been used to save the life of someone I knew, I'm sure I would be delighted. When we don't reject Jesus, but accept that His shed blood has paid the price for our sins, and we allow Him into our lives, I think He must feel overjoyed, and maybe we help Him to feel that the agonising price He paid for us really was worth paying.

Sheep

Sheep aren't the brightest of animals. I suppose to stand in a field all day eating grass they don't need to be, but when it comes to sense they do seem to be particularly lacking.

If you drive across Exmoor you will see them standing or sitting by the side of the road. They have miles of wonderful countryside to roam, eating the grass in perfect safety, and yet they so often choose to eat dust covered grass within feet of passing cars. Another thing they seem to delight in is waiting for cars to get close, then sauntering across the road in front of them. Sometimes it will be just one, but quite often one will start and the others will follow, not surprisingly, like sheep. I suppose it could be that they are more advanced than I am giving them credit for, and that they have a good laugh at bringing all the traffic to a halt, brightening up their day no end. In reality though, it does seem that intelligence, and a sense of self preservation are not things they are endowed with.

They aren't one of the most attractive animals either. Although they are pleasant enough to look at, and a field with sheep in is a very pleasing country scene, they don't have the grace and elegance of a horse, or the lovely faces and attractive markings of cows. When it comes to lambs though, surely they must be some of the most attractive and appealing of any young animals. Whereas watching sheep eat is not really inspiring, watching lambs is totally different. They are so cute and pretty, and to see them gambolling in a field on a sunny spring day gives a lot of pleasure.

As my mother had always enjoyed watching lambs at play, one day I took her to see some at a local farm. At first most of them were either resting or eating, with just a few walking, or maybe running short distances. Occasionally one would run and jump, or kick its back legs in the air, a bit like a miniature bucking bronco. After some minutes though, a few came across to the left of us, fairly close to the gate we were standing at. One looked at us, then another, but they obviously decided we weren't very interesting, and turned away to go off to have fun with their friends.

After just walking around for a minute or two, they decided it was time to run, and went chasing off along the edge of the field, nearly to the end, only to turn round and come chasing back again. A couple more became interested and joined them, and the gallop was repeated, this time with eight lambs involved. The run began to attract attention, and it wasn't long before there were twelve, then fourteen taking part. Every time it was the same. They'd chase down to the end, turn round, and chase back. Sometimes they would stop halfway to have a nose around, before continuing back up the field at speed. There seemed to be no purpose in what they were doing, but I guess a lamb's got to do what a lamb's got to do!

The numbers kept growing, as in two's and three's more came across the field to join in. Eventually there were twenty seven of them in full flight, up and down the field, again and again. It was so funny to watch, and the speed they achieved was amazing. If they'd had fences to jump over it could have been called the Lamb National.

Occasionally one of the sheep would walk across towards them, stop thirty or forty yards away, and then stand there bleating. With some lambs there would be an almost instant response, as one or two of them broke off from the group, and came trotting across to their mother. They would have a quick feed, and then, shortly after, rejoin the others. On another occasion when the mother called, the lamb was obviously having too much fun to come. It was only after several more calls that it finally realised it should go to its mother for food. To me all sheep seem to make virtually the same noise, but it was incredible to see how, with so many animals in that field, the lambs knew which was their mother calling, and went to her. It was also fascinating to see one opportunist lamb go to a sheep for food, only to have the sheep push it away with her nose. The sheep, I presume by smell, knew it wasn't her lamb, so she rejected it, but when her own lambs came they were welcome to feed immediately. Finally, the game was, over, the group broke up, and we went on our way, having received so much pleasure from such a simple thing.

The trouble with human beings is that so often we can be like those lambs. We rush here, there, and everywhere, supposedly trying to achieve things, and get somewhere in life, and yet so often the journey leads nowhere. I once stood on a hill overlooking the M25 motorway, and watched hundreds of cars hurtling along, their occupants all going somewhere, but I wondered how many of those people knew in their lives what the eternal destination was that they were rushing towards. Afterall, that's the most important thing for us all to know.

I know that this life is not all there is, and that when we die it's not the end of the story. I'll talk more about this further on in the book, but will just say now that our souls do go on, and go to face God, though some people can't, or won't accept that. They say, "When you're dead, you're dead", and live their lives accordingly, trying to find purpose, satisfaction and happiness in what they might achieve. Others will recognise that there is something more than just this life, but decide to leave it to the other side of the grave to sort it out, by which time, sadly, it's too late. Again, the personal satisfaction, and a sense of purpose and achievement are what's important, and are going to be attained by effort, hard work, constant busyness, and possessions - they think. Like the lambs they're going flat out to achieve something which won't last, and is going nowhere.

For many lambs their lives are very short. they are born for a purpose, namely to feed people. Those which are kept to grow to adulthood soon lose the fun and boisterousness of youth, and become like their parents, walking slowly around the field, eating grass all day, leading an aimless existence. Many people are like that, going from the freedom of childhood, to following the crowd in the way they go on, getting through their lives, alive, but not really living, missing the purpose filled, satisfying lives they could have. We have been born for a purpose - to know God, and the love He wants to pour into our lives, whether those lives are long or short, and to experience all the good He wants to do for us.

Like those sheep calling their lambs to come to them, God calls us to come to Him. Like the lambs, some people respond as soon as they understand that call, and allow God to feed them with His love, and His peace, and let Him help them to lead fulfilled, purposeful lives. Others, like myself, don't respond straight away, but when they do they are fed, and realise how much good feeding they have been missing out on all the time they were holding back, and resisting the call. Others look in the wrong place. Instead of coming to God through Jesus they will try other things to feed them. Whether it's trying to fill their lives with possessions, being busy or successful, other forms of religion, cults, the occult, or any other alternatives to God, they will never find the lasting inner peace God gives, that only comes from Jesus Christ.

How do I know? Because Jesus said, " I am the way and the truth and the life. No-one comes to the Father, except through Me", and He knew what He was talking about, and what He said was true.

Regrettably, so many in the crowd prefer to stay in the crowd, and not get fed. They either actively reject God, or, even though they are not anti-God, they choose not to respond to His love and call, which amounts to the same thing. Just like the sheep rejecting the lamb which didn't belong to it, when their turn comes to face God He will reject them, because they chose not to accept Jesus, and the forgiveness He offers. They will have forfeited the free gift which Jesus gave His life for to be able to give them. However, all the time there is life it is not too late.

Jesus said, "Ask and it will be given to you, seek and you will find, knock and the door will be opened to you. For everyone who asks receives; he who seeks finds; and to him who knocks, the door will be opened".

Today is the day to stand out from the crowd, to ask, to receive, and to be fed.

Spring

For some people, God doesn't exist. They either can't or won't accept that He's there, and no amount of evidence, no matter how strong, will make them change their minds. For them there can't be a God, and that's the end of it.

Then there are others who think there is some mysterious force behind everything in the universe, out there somewhere, but what it is they don't know. It may be God, but preferably it will be just a nameless force with no identity, because that way it far is more comfortable, as they don't have to be accountable to what is unknown. They certainly don't want the force to be with them.

In both cases, for many of these people, everything that exists is either definitely, or is possibly here by chance. Everything has appeared or evolved, usually in some very implausible way, over millions, or billions of years, but God, or the unnamed force, has not been involved in its creation.

I'm at the other end of the scale, because I do believe in God, and I also believe that He designed and created everything. I believe, not just because I've seen so many, sometimes seemingly impossible answers to prayer, not just because of what He has done in my life, with the peace, the direction, and the help He has given, and so much more, but because of what I see in nature as well. When you look at the night sky, and see so many stars, each keeping to such an accurately defined orbit that it's possible to know where they will be at any time of year, it's phenomenal. When you think of this earth, floating in space, yet always at exactly the right distance from the sun to prevent us burning up or freezing solid, and also having everything on it necessary to sustain life, it's incredible, almost unbelievable.

Scientists tell us, wanting us to believe that what they are saying is an indisputable fact, that the universe started with the big bang, everything being created from an explosion of mysterious gasses which came from a totally unknown source, yet they can't honestly prove any of it. Explosions destroy, they don't, and can't create life, so to say all this order and provision came from an explosion really is the greatest science fiction ever.

If we consider the sun, somehow being able to keep burning constantly over thousands, or, if the scientists are to be believed, millions of years without really decreasing in size, the whole thing is nothing less than miraculous. We often hear the powers that be talking about finding new, sustainable sources of energy, and one existing, and inexhaustible source which is gaining in popularity is solar energy. Even on a cloudy day the sun has the power to provide the energy from 93 million miles away for solar heating to work. Every second of every day, of every year, of every century, the sun continues to burn with such a fiercely intense heat that we can't even begin to imagine it, and yet it never burns out. If this earth suddenly started burning with that intensity, everything would be totally incinerated almost instantly, and this planet would no longer exist, and yet the sun has been burning like that since the solar system was created.

As far as I know, scientists haven't discovered a fuel line into the sun, pumping in gas or oil from some unknown source far out in the galaxy, but somehow, miraculously, the power source of the sun is inextinguishable, and never diminishes. An explosion couldn't do that. An incredible power must have been there at the beginning to put the sun in place with a totally sustainable energy source, and that power was God. The Bible says so, and simple logic confirms that the sun must have had a planned, and miraculous creation.

For me, one of the miracles of this planet is the spring. We know it happens every year, and yet it never ceases to delight and amaze me. Over the winter the trees stand, seemingly lifeless, with their bare branches giving every appearance of being dead, and then suddenly the miracle begins to happen. As the temperature starts to rise the first signs of life appear, and in no time those same trees are covered with fresh green leaves, and look wonderful. No human has told them to do it, and I certainly don't believe they have the intelligence to work it out for themselves. Yet, if we are to believe the scientists, they have evolved that way of going on, somehow realising it was the best way to live, so that every year, just at the right time, the cycle starts all over again.

Suddenly too, the birds know it's time to start nesting. Weeks before their happy event they get busy, collecting whatever they can find to build a desirable, detached residence in which to lay their eggs, and bring up their young. Again, without being told, they put into practise what has been programmed into them, not by a big bang, evolution, or by chance, but by God, the Creator. The chicks hatch, and the parents work so hard collecting the abundance of grubs and insects which are feeding on the abundance of leaves on the trees. Like everything else in nature, everything fits in together perfectly, until man in his wisdom intervenes, and messes things up.

Butterflies have an incredibly complicated development. They start as tiny eggs, which hatch into equally tiny caterpillars. These grow rapidly, and shed their skin several times as they get bigger, and finally fix themselves to a plant with silk before shedding the skin for the final time, under which is a casing called a chrysalis. After one to two weeks, from that chrysalis the butterfly finally emerges, but it then has to fill its limp wings with a fluid, and wait for them to dry before it can fly. That's a very brief explanation, and all that's involved is even more complicated than I've described, but to believe the butterfly was able to work it all out, and be able to evolve in such a way really is illogical. Even human beings couldn't have worked out an evolutionary strategy like that.

Bulbs are equally remarkable. For 11 months or so they lie dormant in the ground until, when their moment arrives, they start to grow. Somehow, those flimsy stalks and leaves, which you break off so easily, force their way up through heavy, solid earth, growing until they've reached their proper height, and then they burst into flower.

Each type has its set time, one of the earliest being snowdrops, then daffodils, bluebells, and so on. I once planted daffodil bulbs very late, not long before they should have been flowering, but they grew, and flowered about 6 weeks behind schedule. However, by the next year they weren't running late. They had automatically adjusted, just like a radio controlled clock, and came up right on time with the others which were there. How did they do it, and how do different bulbs come up at different times? God, who created the universe, who put our constantly burning sun in place, who gave every living creature the knowledge of how to reproduce and survive, cared enough about His creation to even put a time clock in humble bulbs. Now that's attention to detail!

Spring is about new life, a new start, leaving behind the cold and darkness of winter. In our own lives too we can feel as if we are constantly in the grip of winter, or at least in the more unpleasant days autumn can bring, and that there is no way of getting back to the joy and hope of spring. When that happens there is only one answer - we need the Son in our lives. Jesus, the Son of God, the one who never changes, who can never die, whose love can never be extinguished, is the one who can free us from the darkness, from hopelessness, from despair, and give us happiness and a bright future. Jesus said, "I am making everything new", and that's what He wants to do in our lives. When we allow the Son to shine in our lives He gives us light, comfort, help, and so much more.

The birds need an abundance of food to feed their hungry chicks, and it's provided for them. Jesus said He came to give us life, and give it to the full, and He wants to give us an abundance of all we need to have that.

Looking at it logically, with bulbs it would seem impossible for such flimsy stalks and leaves to be able to push their way through the soil, but with God nothing is impossible, and somehow He gave them the capability to get into the light, and flourish. Sometimes it can seem that the cares of this world are on top of us, just as heavy as the soil is for the bulbs, and that there is no way forward, or up. We can't see how we can find any light, or be able to flourish, but even if we can't see a way forward, there always is one, Jesus knows it, and for Him nothing is impossible. He said, "Come to Me, all you who are weary and burdened, and I will give you rest". He went on to say, "You will find rest for your souls".

Spring is about new life, and renewal, and there's the hope and expectation of what's to come. Whether we are in the spring, summer, autumn, or even the last few days of winter in our lives, Jesus offers us rest for our souls. He offers us a new life, renewal, a way forward, the hope and expectation of what's to come, and the most beautiful eternal spring we could ever imagine.

The Inferiority Complex

Before I started school I've been told that I was very confident at talking to people. Apparently I would stand and talk to the lady next door without any problems, and it seems there was no difficulty for me in being able to do that with anyone. However, when I started school, through different things that happened, it all changed. I lost confidence, and became painfully shy, and that affected me in every area of life. If we were playing at home and the ball went into the next door neighbour's garden, I would always ask my brother to go to ask for it back, and if he refused, and I had to go it was such a hard thing to do. The neighbours were nice people, but it was still so hard. For anyone who's never had that problem it may seem difficult to understand, but when you are like that it's horrible.

That also gave me a huge inferiority complex which continued for many years, and to compensate I wanted to impress the other pupils, and, as I grew older, adults too, although I probably never succeeded. In my late teens I wanted to be a Formula 1 racing driver, mainly because I really would love to have raced, but also because if I had become one, and been successful, those I'd been to school with would have seen me, and hopefully been impressed. They would possibly have said, "That's Jeremy Bishopp, I went to school with him." I would never have known whether they did or not, but that was my thinking. Looking back as I grew older I realised how foolish it was, but that's what inferiority can do for you. I never did race at any level, which is probably just as well, as it was at a time when so many drivers were being killed every year, and I may well have been one of them. The reason I didn't even try to do it though was because of the way I was, as I just didn't have the confidence to really pursue what I would love to have done.

The trouble with feeling this inferiority is that it can last a life time. When I had worked for other people I had always been successful in whatever I did, and when I then started my own business it far exceeded my expectations of all that I'd hoped to achieve. The problem was, that no matter what I did, the inferiority complex was still there. Because whatever work I'd done had always involved dealing with numerous people, the shyness had largely, though not completely been overcome, but the sense of inferiority wouldn't go away. Money and success couldn't get rid of it, nor could anything else. Even as I turned 40 it was still there, and I was still wanting to impress. When I played badminton I would try hard, hoping that the others there would think I was playing well, although invariably I wasn't.

By this time I'd sold my business, and started another one, which again was going well. I'd also become a Christian a few years earlier, but even that hadn't taken away the problem. I've said in another story though that God doesn't deal with everything in us that needs to be changed all at once, it's a bit at a time. He knows when the time is right for each thing to be dealt with, and that we're now ready to respond to what He wants to do to help us.

At work one morning I was really struggling with my sense of inferiority, finding it very hard, when suddenly God spoke to me so clearly. Now that may seem a strange thing to say, but this is not about hearing weird, harmful, or sinister voices which some people are sadly plagued by. Many Christians do hear from God, because God is real, and definitely does speak to those who follow Him. He spoke so clearly to the prophets in the Bible, telling them what would happen, and those things they heard came true. God can speak audibly, sometimes it can be in our heads in a way that's so loud it's almost audible, which once happened to me, sometimes it can be almost in a whisper. Sometimes it can be through words in the Bible, or through other Christians He's given a message to for us. Whichever way it comes, when it's from God it will be accurate and relevant, it won't be harmful, it will be proved to be true, and we'll know without doubt it's from Him.

This particular morning, in the midst of all my struggles, and even though I hadn't been expecting it, God suddenly spoke to me so clearly and gently, and I knew it was from Him. All God said was, "You don't have to prove yourself to me."

Those few words changed my life. Almighty God, the all powerful creator of the universe, who knows me inside out, with all my faults and failings, cared about my situation so much, because He loves me so much, that He brought transformation. As those words went through my mind, I suddenly realised their significance, and thought, "If I don't have to prove myself to God, I don't have to prove myself to anyone," and that's true, because I don't. From then on things were different. When I played badminton I was able to relax, and play to enjoy myself, not to try to impress. Also, to my surprise, my playing improved significantly, and when I got it wrong it really didn't matter, and certainly didn't give me an inferiority complex.

Not having to prove myself to other people doesn't mean that I don't care about them and their feelings, and what they think about things, because I do care. I like to be friendly, to be nice to them, and I don't want to cause anyone hurt in any way, but it's not because I'm desperately wanting them to think well of me, it's not that I want to impress. It's because I'm free to be who God wants me to be, and I don't have to try to reach certain standards to gain other people's approval or acceptance of me. God said I don't have to prove myself to Him, and that's all I need, and that's what everyone needs who is suffering from an inferiority complex. The good news is that what He said to me doesn't just apply to me, it applies to everyone on this planet, because He loves each one of us equally. We don't need to reach a certain standard for God's approval, we just need to come to Him, and let Him set us free.

The Carpenter

Some people have the ability and gifting to make things which are not only functional, but are also attractive, or even beautiful, as well. Whether they work in wood, metal, clay, or other materials, they can skilfully fashion items from them which are are good and pleasing to look at. Others are able to take a blank canvas, and draw or paint beautiful pictures which give pleasure to many.

Many years ago now, my father made a dining room table which was strong, totally fit for the purpose, and also extremely attractive to look at. He put time, and a lot of care into making it, and the result was very good. The table has had a great deal of use over the years, and, apart from a few marks from wear and tear, it is as good as ever. We have now inherited it, and today it still gives me as much pleasure to see it and use it as it has always done. He also made a number of wooden bowls by first gluing blocks of wood of different colours together, and then carefully turned them on a lathe. Finally, they would be polished, and once more the results were good, and very attractive, and, again, they are still in use today. He'd had very little training, but somehow he had the ability to do so many things well. I would love to say that I have inherited that gifting, and that everything practical I turn my hand to is a success, but unfortunately I can't.

When I was at school, all the boys in the woodwork class were given the opportunity to make something of our choosing, and I decided I wanted to make a case for a base drum. At the time I didn't have a drum kit, but I thought I would make the case in preparation for the time when I did have one.

With instruction from the teacher I set to work, and finally, after much effort, the case was finished, and it really was something to see. The way I had filled up the gaps that were there in most of the dovetail joints with sawdust and glue was a work of art. Yes, I know dovetail joints are supposed to fit perfectly to give the strength, but my ingenuity and skill in filling the gaps in this way proved to be just as effective, and the case held together without any problems. The thing is, joints which fit perfectly really have no character, and always having gaps in the joints I did in woodwork had definitely become my trademark. It's possibly the reason though that my teacher felt it wouldn't be worth me taking what then was the GCE 'O' Level exam in the subject, and I know he was right in that.

However, the drum case was duly taken home, and was then put in the loft, in preparation for the arrival of the drum kit. It stayed there for a long time, and was used to store papers in. With a move to another house it went to another loft, still used for the same papers, and still waiting for me to buy the drum kit. Eventually, many years later, I finally bought a drum kit, and at last the case was ready to be used for what I had intended it for. Unfortunately, unlike the dining room table my father had made which was fit for purpose, my case wasn't.

The problem with making a drum case without having a drum kit was that I didn't know the measurements of a base drum. In spite of my skill with sawdust and glue, I hadn't thought to find out from anywhere else either what size the drum would be. To my mind, the size of the case I was making seemed more than adequate. When I did get the kit, and looked at the case, I realised that it was not only the wrong size, it was the wrong shape as well, and the drum wouldn't go in. The only good thing was that the sawdust and glue were still working well! The case stayed in the loft, woodworm managed to find it, and eventually it went on a bonfire. Thinking about it now, I may well have missed an opportunity, as I should have entered it for the Turner Prize as a so called work of art, called it 'Shattered Dreams', and I would probably have made a fortune! Alas, it's too late for that now.

Even today, it would be pointless for me to train as a carpenter, as I know that ability just isn't there, I would still mess things up, and still need a ready supply of sawdust and glue! In contrast, a skilled carpenter can make things of beauty which work as intended, and can sometimes last for centuries, and it must be very satisfying to be able to do that.

When Jesus was alive, before He began His ministry of reaching out to the people of Israel with the good news of forgiveness and love, He had trained and worked as a carpenter. He must have known what it was like to take a rough piece of wood, and skilfully transform it into something new by cutting, joining, smoothing, and polishing it.

To have earned His living in this way, He would have had to be very good at what He did, especially without having the use of the modern precision tools which are available today. As a skilled carpenter He would have been able to look at a piece of wood and see the potential in it to make something useful, even if to the untrained eyes of others there appeared to be nothing of worth or value there at all.

What Jesus has always been an expert at as well though, is changing people's lives, and making them into something much better. It doesn't matter what people's lives may be like, even if they feel theirs is very rough. When people allow Him to come into their lives to help them, He is able to take all the roughness, and everything that's not right, and with great care, gently change them. He can mould and polish them, and make their lives into something special. Even if we think we have no value, and sadly many people do feel like that, or if other people look at us and think that about us too, Jesus sees us differently. We may feel we're useless, or can't do anything, or we may have been made to feel that way by others, but Jesus sees the potential in us, and He sees below the surface to what nobody else sees, and to what sometimes we don't see either.

Unlike me with the carpentry, it may be that we think we're pretty good, and don't mess up very often, although we know there have been times when we have done things wrong, and there are still times when that happens. If you're anything like me, it's on a daily basis. Unlike me too, trying to make the best of a bad job with sawdust and glue, Jesus doesn't just want to patch us up by giving each of us a cheap veneer. If you've ever watched an expert on the Antiques Roadshow enthusing about a piece of furniture, you will have seen that when they look at the back of an item, which would normally be hidden from view against a wall, and they find that it's been as carefully and lovingly made as the part which is always on view, they know that a real craftsman has put his heart into making it. Everything has been made perfectly, because he cared so much about it, and what he did had to be the best. That's what Jesus wants to do for us, because He cares so much about each one of us.

If we'll let Him, because He knows we really do have great value, Jesus can make our lives shine and be beautiful from the inside out. Our lives can become a thing of beauty from whichever angle people see us. The question is, do we want to let Him help us and bless us, and put things right, or do we want to keep trying to hold our lives together with sawdust and glue?

Brambles, nettles, and other undesirables

For many years my mother had a fairly large garden, and a lot of it was comprised of lawns and bushes, so it could be controlled fairly easily, if it had regular attention. In it were two cherry trees which were absolutely beautiful when they flowered in the spring, several buddleias, a large forsythia bush, and various other flowering shrubs and trees, all of which added beauty. In one part she had a greenhouse, with a lawn in front, so that part was fine too. Behind it though was another matter, because there she had a small strip of rough ground, with a steep bank rising from it, which had remained uncultivated, as it was quite difficult to deal with.

For a long time that part hadn't been too much of a problem, but some years ago things changed, and the brambles and nettles started to get a real hold. We suddenly realised how much growth they had put on, without us noticing what was happening. The brambles had not only crawled along the ground, they were also working their way up the greenhouse, clinging to the frame, and starting to cut out the light. If they had been left, in time the whole structure would have been covered, and the inside filled too, as they were starting to work their way through small gaps between the glass and the frame. The nettles too, with their vicious stings, were flourishing, filling in the spaces between the brambles, making the whole area an impenetrable, and well protected mess. Something had to be done, but how?

The problem, as I stood there, protected by gardening gloves, and ready to begin, was where did I start with this seemingly impossible task? There was just so much of it, and whereas ideally I would like to have gone right to the centre, to pull out the brambles by their roots, it just couldn't be done. Instead I had to start from the outside, gradually working my way in, cutting off each tendril one at a time, throwing them into a pile to be burnt later. It was a hard job, but slowly I made progress, pulling out roots of brambles and nettles as

I reached them, until finally the ground was clear. Having opened it up so much though the light showed up another problem, as the insidious old man's beard had been doing its destructive work undetected. In various places, covered by the other weeds, it had grown up into the trees and bushes on the bank, holding on firmly, and left unchecked, in time it would have killed them. Near the roots, the thickness of the creeping tentacles of some of them was amazing. Working away out of sight they had become firmly established, and at times a saw was needed to cut them off. The roots were so deep that it was impossible to get everything out without a huge amount of effort in digging some very large holes, so I decided it was better to keep a check in future, and cut them off when they started to grow again. The trouble was though, by doing that, I had literally not dealt with the root cause. Also, my good intentions weren't followed up as often as they should have been, and so in time more hard work was needed.

It had seemed such a huge job when I started, but gradually, with perseverance I finally achieved my goal of clearing the area. I had to cut out a bit at a time, dealing with the easier parts first, then reaching deep seated problem areas, removing them, and moving again, steadily and constantly clearing out the rubbish. As I worked, I could see that that is such a good illustration of how God works with us when He is in our lives, and that's just what He did with me.

Knowing my fears about what I thought would happen if I did become a Christian, as I've previously explained in the 'Umbrellas' story, when I finally took the step of accepting Jesus as my Saviour nothing appeared to have happened at all. It wasn't an emotional experience, I didn't feel any different, everything seemed just the same. It wasn't until about a fortnight later that I suddenly realised God had been working in my life since that night, changing me very gently and quietly, and I knew nothing about it. What I also hadn't realised then was that God loves us totally, He works things out perfectly, that He understood my situation, and knew exactly where to begin. Let me explain what happened.

I used to have a business supplying DIY shops, and I was always in a hurry to get from one customer to the next, because the more people I called on, the more money I would make. I would drive fast, I thought everybody else on the road was an idiot, they wouldn't get out of my way, and the frustration was huge, and getting worse. I knew it was harming me, but no matter how much I told myself to change, I couldn't. Having been a Christian for that short time, one day in South London, in my usual hurry, I drove into a one way street, and there in front of me, with cars parked on either side, was a milk float crawling along. There was no way past, and my usual reaction would have been to go berserk, but God had been busy, gently, and lovingly starting to change my life. Instead of anger and frustration, quite unexpectedly I started to laugh. There was nothing I could do but crawl along too, and yet I could see the funny side of it, and there was no anger or frustration.

That incident was a defining moment in my Christian life, because through it I realised that God can be trusted totally. He knew my fears, and when I finally decided to trust Him, He didn't abuse that trust. Instead, quietly, and perfectly, God started working in my life, until that moment when He knew I was ready to start experiencing

His love. From that moment on I was then not only willing to let Him change anything that needed changing, I asked Him to. Just like me cutting away the brambles and nettles a bit at a time, God has been dealing with me over the years a bit at a time. Some things He's dealt with quickly, others have taken much longer. Like the old man's beard, hidden away, and deeply rooted, there have been things which have suddenly come to light, rooted deeply in the past, and almost forgotten about, but God hadn't forgotten. His timing is perfect, and at the right time He has shown that they need dealing with. Unlike me leaving the roots in the ground because it was too hard, nothing is too hard for God, and He is able to reach even the deepest roots, and remove the problem.

As I didn't deal with them constantly, and thoroughly, the weeds grew back again, because that's the way weeds are. If my mother's garden had then been left unattended for years it would have been covered with all manner of weeds, and become a total wilderness. Every beautiful plant and shrub would have been choked and killed, leaving nothing lovely at all. We can be like that too. When we keep God at bay, and refuse the constant attention He wants to give to help us, the choking weeds we allow in during our lives can't be dealt with, no matter how hard we may try. Instead of having peace, contentment and freedom in our spirit, we're held firmly, with the tentacles of the past gripping us ever tighter, and refusing to let go.

After all these years, God still has work to do in me, and I know I will never be perfect. Thankfully, God understands everything, and He knows I am still very much a flawed human being, but He loves me anyway, He's at work, He never gives up on me, and He's still changing me. Even as I have been writing this, I have experienced a fresh appreciation of what God did for me those many years ago now, when He poured His love into me, and showed me how much He cares. I don't deserve His love, but I'm so very grateful I have it. I trust Him, because He has shown me He is totally trustworthy, and I'm very happy to let Him continue clearing out the rubbish in my life whenever it appears, because through that there is freedom, there is release, and a life that's worth living.

Rejection

It would be great to think that no-one has ever been hurt or harmed by rejection, and we can all sail through life without any damage having been done, but sadly, that isn't the case. It's almost certain that everyone who's ever lived has suffered rejection of some sort, and that continues to be the case. Sometimes it can be small, and the person affected is able to shrug it off and not be bothered by it at all, but at other times it can cause so much damage that it lasts a life time.

A lady I know has given me permission to write about her situation, and the long term damage which began early in her life. As a young child life was normal, but then her parents split up when she was three years old, and suddenly she no longer saw her mother. At that age she couldn't understand what had happened, and for her it seemed that her mother had rejected her. The short term result was that she didn't speak for 6 weeks, but the long term effect continued for many years. Making, and keeping friends at school was difficult, and that carried on into adulthood, because the fear of rejection meant not allowing others to get too close in case the pain came again. The lack of close friends continued to fuel that whole sense of being rejected. That reaction is very common in those who have been damaged by rejection, however it may have come, and from whatever the source may have been.

Rejection by parents is extremely harmful, and it can take many forms. It's recognised that even in the womb the unborn baby can sense emotions which can affect it in life significantly. If a mother is wanting a girl, and finds she's having a boy, or is having a girl and wanted a boy, and makes it clear how unhappy she is about it, the baby can sense those emotions. Physically attached to the mother, even before the child is born, rejection has been fed in, which will affect their life. Too often these days the father of a child will walk away from the relationship with the mother thinking it doesn't matter, but it does. The child is left feeling totally rejected because the father didn't want them, and didn't care.

If parents tell a child they're stupid, or ugly, that they are a failure, or that they will never amount to anything, or any other hurtful things they may say, that's a huge rejection coming from the ones the child is looking to for love. It leaves children very damaged, feeling they are the ones who are wrong, they will reject themselves because they believe it, and in turn reject others. If at an early age a child's parent, or brother or sister dies, that child can feel rejected, as they don't understand the real significance at that stage, and think that the person has gone away and left them.

There are so many other things which can cause rejection. Being called names by other children at school, as well as being hurtful, can make someone feel that that is what they are like, that is what they are, and that false, and unkind image can stay with them for life. Being rejected for promotion at work, being rejected in a relationship, or in countless other ways, can make people feel a failure. Through any of these things people can lose respect for themselves, and may even hate themselves. It can affect their decisions, cover up their gifts and abilities so that they're not used, and rob them of their potential. Instead, they will believe and live out the wrong things that have been fed in. They can't be themselves because of the fear of being rejected, and they will reject other people as well so that they won't be rejected. It can even cause physical sickness.

Now that's a pretty depressing list of things, and it's not exhaustive, but there is good news, because no-one has to be trapped like that for life. Jesus knows exactly what it's like to be rejected, because His rejection was far greater than anyone who's ever lived. As the Son of God, He was rejected by the religious leaders, by many in the population, and by the Romans. He was even rejected by one of His disciples (one of His followers) who'd been with Him for three years, but who then betrayed Him, resulting in Jesus being crucified. When He needed their support most He was also rejected by the rest of His twelve disciples, who fled when He was arrested, leaving Him alone to face the mob who'd come for Him, although they did come back later when it was too late to help. So Jesus knows how hard it is, and what rejection can do to us, and He understands totally.

Having said that, when you're suffering from rejection it can be hard to believe that God or Jesus could accept you and love you. In what is the most famous prayer in the world, which is known as the Lord's prayer, it begins, 'Our Father in heaven', and many times in the New Testament God is referred to as being our Father, that is, our heavenly Father. The trouble is, for many people that can be hard to accept. When people have had an abusive father, or a violent one, if he had punished them unfairly, shown them no love, or rejected them and walked away forever, or in any other way had been less than a father should be, then it's very hard to accept that God is a God of love. It's very easy then to feel that they would be rejected by God, and that He would treat them in a similar way too, although, in reality, the opposite of that is definitely true.

Even if people have had great parents it can still be hard to trust God, and be willing to accept His help. Whatever brought the rejection, that protective shield that's been put up, and been in place for so long, keeping others at bay, can be used in just the same way to keep God at a distance. The fear of rejection can be just as great, and yet, as I've said previously, God loves us all so much that he sent Jesus to die for us. That great love won't let Him reject us. Just to confirm the truth of that, in what is called Luke's Gospel, (chapter 9, verse 22), Jesus, when talking to His disciples about Himself said, "The Son of Man must suffer many things, and be rejected by the elders, chief priests and teachers of the law, and He must be killed, and on the third day be raised to life." The Son of Man was one of the titles for Jesus, and as God in human form He knew He would be rejected and killed for us, and that's why I can say without any doubt that God will never reject anyone on this earth when they come to Him. That's guaranteed.

The lady I spoke of at the beginning had had a hard road to travel, but when, in spite of all the rejection, she was able to allow Jesus into her life, and trust God for His help, it was then that she began to start moving forward on the road to freedom. A lot of help was needed, and it came a bit at a time, gently and lovingly, in the timing God knew was right to bring her release and wholeness.

When we can accept God as He really is, the God of love, and not keep Him at a distance, but allow Him to help us, we can then begin to accept ourselves, and believe in ourselves. God can restore us, He can heal the past, free us from the darkness and oppression of rejection, turn our lives around, and give us a new and bright future. We just need to take the shield down, and let God show us that He will never reject us, He will never forsake us, He will never take His love away from us.

The Concert

Some years ago my wife and I had the opportunity to join the beginner's section of the local silver band. For a long time we had played other instruments in church, Jane on the flute, and me on the drums, but this was something totally different. Jane began learning to play the euphonium, a complete contrast to the flute, and I chose the trombone, something I had wanted to do for many years.

We steadily progressed, and eventually reached the point where the novices were to play some pieces in a concert being given by the senior band. That came and went, as did further concerts, without too much trauma, and each time we seemed to get through them reasonably competently. The audiences would clap, either out of kindness or sympathy, and we would finish, very relieved that the performance had not been a disaster. That is, until we came to the Christmas concert.

For weeks we had been practising Christmas songs, and I had been playing them quite confidently. In one particular number, as one of the four trombonists, I seemed to be the one taking the lead, and, if the others weren't sure, they were following me. There was one part in it, about two thirds of the way through, where the trombones were the only ones playing the melody, whilst all the other instruments played the backing. Every time, I would get the timing right, and end up fairly pleased with the way it had gone. The evening approached.

On the night of the concert the hall was completely full, and eventually our turn came to face the audience. The first song went quite well, and then we came to the one I've just mentioned. Everything was fine, but as we neared our main part I completely lost where I was. Rather than have the embarrassment of sitting there doing nothing, I decided I would fake it. I moved the slide to different positions, sometimes playing a note, but mostly keeping silent, trying to give the appearance that I was playing what I was supposed to. That may well have worked if it hadn't been for the fact that the other three had totally lost it too, and they didn't know where they were either! We finally came to the end, and I managed to play the last note on time! The audience were kind enough to clap, but what should have been a very enjoyable piece to play had been awful, and we were left feeling extremely uncomfortable.

Afterwards, I spoke to one of the other so called trombonists, and told him that I had been faking it, to which he replied that his problem was that he had been trying to follow my bluffs! I later spoke to the conductor, and he was very kind and understanding about it, but the trouble was, whereas we hoped the audience may not have realised how wrong it had gone, he knew. If it had just been me who was wrong he may not have realised, but we were all wrong, and for a while the poor man was conducting no melody at all. Thankfully, it was a small village event, with about 120 people there, and only four of those in the audience knew us, so the embarrassment was short lived. Life can be like that though, but the consequences are far more serious.

Many people today are out of time with God, and they are as lost as I was in that song. They will try all sorts of ways to make life work, often putting on a front, hoping to appear to others that everything is alright. Or they will attempt to keep in step with other people, but the difficulty is, so often those people are trying desperately to keep in step as well.

Particularly in the western world, those who choose to keep out of step with God far outnumber those who choose to follow Him, but are they right? As I look at the world today it is so obvious that the more people have turned away from God, the more society has been breaking down, and the unhappier people have become. It is very hard these days to find anyone who is really satisfied with life, or who is not worried about so many of the things we see going on all around us. Just as in our piece of music, when we are out of time with God, unity and harmony goes, and the result is an unhappy mess. The majority may have decided not to follow God, but what is happening in so many lives shows that the majority are out of tune.

To anyone who didn't know, the four of us were all apparently getting it right, but unfortunately, the conductor knew. It amazes me how conductors can follow what so many different instruments should be doing, and can tell when a particular musician is getting it wrong. To me it doesn't seem possible, but they do it. Since I started playing I have also realised how essential the conductor is, not only in the rehearsals to say what he or she wants done, but in the actual performance too. In the past, when I was watching a professional orchestra I used to assume that, as they were so well rehearsed, they could manage very well without the conductor for the performance, but that's not so. Even though they are excellent musicians, without the conductor the music would not sound as good, and so much could go wrong. He has the ability to hear everything that's going on, to keep everyone united, and to get the best possible results.

What amazes me even more though is that God knows everyone who is alive on this planet today. How He does it I don't know, but He does. He knows those who are deliberately out of step with Him, and want to stay that way. He knows those who are out of step, but would like to know Him, and He knows those who are in step with Him, and want to follow His leading. Even more, He loves everyone on this planet equally.

The problem for us is that, because God knows everything about us, we can't fake it with Him. It's no good pretending we're better than we are, that we're getting it right, or that He will miss it when we get it wrong because we'll be hidden by so many others. He knows it all. A further problem is that this life is not a rehearsal, it's the real thing. It's not the case that when we die, and go to face God, we can get in tune then, and 'it'll be alright on the night', because it won't. We have to get in step with God now. Jesus made it very clear that if we leave it until the next life it's too late. God is the One who can direct us in the very best way to go in every area of our lives, and He can keep us in tune, but we need to let Him lead us today.

If I hadn't lost where I was that night everything could have been very different, but, in the long term, it doesn't matter at all. It was just a small concert, and really, so unimportant. I may be in the minority, but if I had missed following God, everything would have been completely different. I wouldn't have the inner peace I have now, or the joy, or the love, or the assurance that when I die I will be with God forever, in spite of all the things I've done wrong, or messed up. That would have mattered totally, because it's so important. I have never regretted getting in step with God, and being under His guidance. Would now be the time for you to get in step with God too?

Niagara Falls

For me, one of the most spectacular sights I have ever seen is Niagara Falls. From the American side of the river what you can see of the top of their falls is fairly impressive, but when I saw it, it was certainly not what I was hoping for, or expecting. However, cross the bridge over the river into Canada, and you then have, literally, a totally different view of things. As you turn left, and drive along the road, you are greeted by the sight of the whole of the American Falls, and then you begin to be impressed, but more is to come. Just a little further on and you suddenly see the wonderful sight of the Horseshoe Falls, standing there in all their glory, to the delight of the Canadians, in whose territory they stand.

I have been fortunate enough to go there on three occasions, and I have seen the Falls from every way of looking at them. I stayed in a hotel where every bedroom looked out over them, I have been down in the lift to the viewing area at the base of the Falls, I have watched them tirelessly from the path at the top of the Horseshoe Falls, and I have twice been on the Maid of the Mist boats which go very close to the base of the Falls. As well as this, I have seen them from the very high vantage point of the Skylon Tower, which rises hundreds of feet over the town which has grown up around the Falls, and I have been over them in a helicopter. I have not risked going over on a tightrope, as Blondin did, and I have not been over them in a barrel, as my enthusiasm does not stretch that far, but, apart from that, my delight in the grandeur of the Falls knows no bounds. Even now, having spent so much time there, if I ever have the chance to go again I will certainly take it. A man I met who worked there daily said he never tired of seeing them, and I can believe that.

As well as seeing them in all these ways, I have also seen them in different weather situations. From May onwards, the clear water, with its beautiful greeny blue colour, flows freely, with incredible power, in summer the flow being an amazing 646,000 gallons a second. How it's possible to measure this I don't know. I imagined men standing in the river with buckets, hurriedly scooping the water up, but they would of course need lots of men, and lots of buckets, so I expect they have resorted to the use of modern technology instead. It's a shame, because I think my idea is better, but that's progress for you.

In winter the flow is greatly reduced because of the ice further up river, and it is not until about mid May that the river is clear, and the boats are then able to start making their continuous trips to the Falls. I have seen ice breakers, one American and one Canadian, working together constantly, to break up the packs of ice which come right up to the water's edge. Back at the Falls the result of their work can be seen and heard, as huge lumps of ice crash down into the river basin below. Whatever the situation, the Falls are awesome, and it is incredible that, day after day, and year after year, the water just keeps flowing. Long after I left them far behind, the water still flows relentlessly on.

One slightly sad thing is that the Falls are changing, imperceptibly, but surely. Every year, because of erosion, the Horseshoe Falls retreat by about an inch. Now that is obviously very little, and it's amazing that all that water doesn't wear the rocks away much faster, but since I was last there, they will be twenty three inches further back. Eventually, if the world lasts that long, these beautiful Falls will be no more. Whether it is technological progress, or whether it is the things of nature, everything changes, and, in time, so much passes into history.

Going to Niagara made me realise more than I did already just how immense the power of God is. Those Falls have huge power, but God put them in place, and that's just a small part of what He did in creating this universe. As I said in a previous chapter, I know many people these days believe the scientists with their theories about the 'big bang', thinking that because they are scientists they must be right, but to me it just doesn't make sense. How can gasses coming together and exploding create something as diverse and as beautiful as this planet? Everything we need to sustain a good quality of life has been provided, and I don't believe that gasses could work that miracle. I know this world isn't perfect, but it's man who has messed it up. Niagara Falls are wonderful, but the man made town there is tacky, and not worth seeing, and I could never eulogise over that.

If people are really determined to convince themselves that God doesn't exist, then they will listen to one or more of the many, ever changing theories that the scientists put forward, and accept it as truth, and absolute fact. I heard on the radio a man expounding his belief that life began on this planet by micro organisms travelling to earth in meteorites from Mars, then finding just the right conditions to grow. He didn't explain though how he could know they were on Mars, and how, also, they managed to survive the incredibly high temperatures as they came through the earth's atmosphere which must have killed them if they were there at all. How they could have developed into elephants, fish, birds, human beings, and so much else I don't know, and neither did he, but for him it was no doubt more comforting to believe in that, than face up to the fact that God does exist, and that one day, like it or not, and in spite of not wanting to believe, he will have to face God.

I have seen scientists on television desperately trying to prove that God doesn't exist, showing, as far as they are concerned, that He was not involved in creating this or that particular area of life. Amazingly, no matter how hard they tried to take God out of the equation, there were always areas that they couldn't quite explain, or cope with, to prove they were right.. To me it was obvious - God is in it. In spite of not being able to find what they were hoping to, the existence of God was still something they were not prepared to acknowledge, or look for. The odds of this planet having everything provided for life in every form to exist has been calculated, by scientists, no less, as being between very many millions, and 1 in 7 quintillion (that's 7 with 20 zeros after it)! Yet still they are determined to say we're here by chance. If you are determined not to find God at any price, I guarantee you won't find Him.

Of course, I realise that I could be accused of believing in God, even though all the supposed scientific 'wisdom' cries, "No, don't do it," and tries to tell me not to. As I look at creation though, with all its vast diversity, beauty, and order, even though I don't understand how there can be a God, or where He came from, I have no option but to say that the evidence all around us proclaims that God is real, He does exist. The water at Niagara, in other rivers, and in the seas never stops moving, we use it to sustain life, as well as a multitude of other purposes, it evaporates, then returns to earth, and yet, miraculously, the amount of water on the planet always stays the same. It is not gradually increasing or decreasing - how could an explosion of gasses work that miracle?

No scientist, no matter how brilliant, could create, from nothing, tiny living cells, and turn them into every type of creature that exists on this planet, but, unbelievably, they claim that's what the miraculous gasses did. Every creature knows exactly how to breed and care for their young, even though the diversity in them all is staggering, but it's all programmed in, they do it automatically, nobody has had to tell them, and neither have the 'miraculous gasses'. Even Darwin, with his theory of evolution, (and we should recognise that it is only his theory, not fact), acknowledged before he died that the human eye was much too complex to have evolved. That was before modern technology showed that the eye is even more complex than he thought it was, but people do seem to keep very quiet about that today. The miraculous gasses couldn't do it, but the scientists won't admit to it.

There is one final thing that I don't believe any gas, no matter how clever, could give a human being, and that is what we call our soul, It is impossible to evolve a soul, and yet every one has one. No doctor can find it by scans, but it is there. It is that part of us, the real us, the part that makes us what we are, that does not die when our earthly bodies do. It is the part that goes on beyond death to face God. So many people around the world have had after death experiences of travelling towards a bright light, even of meeting Jesus, and it is the soul that makes that journey. I believe that bright light is where God is, and no miraculous gas can have made something evolve which is beyond human understanding. I'll talk more about the soul in a later story.

Niagara Falls are beautiful, but they can be deadly, as, sadly, many people have found. When our souls make that final journey towards God, and, whether we want to or not, we will all have to do it, if Jesus is our Saviour, and is there to receive us, it will be a beautiful journey, and a great welcome to look forward to. Unlike the things of this world, God's kingdom will never pass away. It will always be perfection, we will always have perfect peace, and everlasting joy. If He is not our Saviour, it will be more terrifying than the power of Niagara Falls could ever be.

Twigs

Walking up to the local woods one spring morning, shortly before Easter, I had to walk up a rough, tree lined road to reach them. At one point I heard a van some way behind me, and so moved over to the side to let it pass. As I waited for it I looked down, and on the ground were two twigs forming a perfect cross as they lay there. As a Christian, for me the cross has a huge significance, because Jesus was crucified, and died on a cross, to take away my sins, and the sins of the world. He paid the price we should pay by giving His life for us on that cross. Two insignificant twigs were a reminder of that event, and it was good to see a cross, just as, on some rare occasions, I've seen and appreciated a cross in the sky made by the vapour trails of two planes. Those crosses have no mystic, supernatural power, they are just reminders of the death of Jesus.

As I stood there looking at them, the van came past me and ran over the twigs, totally destroying the cross. I'm sure the driver didn't realise what he had done, as, even if he had seen them on the road, which I doubt very much, two small twigs are hardly something to be avoided. If he had been so sharp eyed that he had seen them forming a cross it probably wouldn't have meant anything to him, and I certainly wouldn't have expected him to swerve to avoid them. He drove on, the cross was gone, and so was that moment I'd appreciated, and I continued my walk.

As I thought about what had happened, I could see that it is exactly what people have been doing to Jesus for nearly 2,000 years now. Jesus, the Son of God, came to earth preaching a message of peace and joy, love and forgiveness, telling people that following God's ways and plans was the right way to go. He told them they should turn from their sins, ask for forgiveness, allow God to heal and restore broken lives, and to begin a new and better way of living.

For many of the people who heard Him, they found the thought of following God, rather than being able to continue with their sins the way they wanted to, totally repulsive, so just like those twigs, they would gladly have trampled Jesus into the dust and destroyed Him, if they had been able to get away with it. For them, they found His message very uncomfortable, because He was shining the light on what was wrong with their lives. They preferred to be angry with Him, and hate Him, rather than see that what He was wanting to do was to bless them, and give them happy, fulfilled lives.

For others they didn't hate Him or want Him dead, but, just like the van driver, they didn't see what some people could see. For them He was just another travelling preacher who had nothing to say that they wanted to listen to, and so they walked away and ignored Him. Jesus performed miracle after miracle, showing that He was the Son of God, but for them the miracles weren't enough to believe in Him, to see the truth, and to follow Him. For them He was as insignificant as two small twigs on the ground.

For yet others they did see who Jesus was. He was there, right in front of them, but instead of stopping, listening to Him, and then accepting what He had to say, of how He wanted to bless them, and give them the gift of eternal life, they chose to swerve out the way, and carry on. They chose to go their own way, and leave the One with the truth, and the words of eternal life behind. Sadly, instead of stopping, then following His way, they chose the road that led to destruction, just as surely as the van driver would have done if he'd swerved and crashed. For him it may just have been his van that was destroyed. For them it was the gift of eternal life with God which was destroyed.

Some did see who He was, they decided to stop and listen, and just like me being happy to spend time stopping and looking at that cross because of what the cross stands for, they were happy and eager to spend time in His presence. They saw that what He said was true, that because He was, and is, the Son of God, He was able to change their lives in good ways, and they decided to accept that free gift He was offering. Compared to the other groups though, those who did choose to follow Him were very much in the minority. Letting go of old, engrained habits, their old way of life, and starting anew was too uncomfortable for most people to accept, and they continued to go their own way.

The final group was the religious leaders of the day, as they not only refused to believe who Jesus was, they also totally rejected Him, and they hated Him. It didn't matter what He said, or how many miracles He performed, they were absolutely determined not to accept Him, and instead to condemn Him of being guilty of blasphemy. If the van driver had seen the cross, and wanted to destroy it, he had the power to do it, and could have made a conscious decision to run over it. Unlike the first group I mentioned who hated Jesus, but weren't able to trample Him to death, the religious leaders had the power to have Jesus killed, and they chose to use it. They wanted Jesus totally destroyed.

Through their influence with a man called Pontius Pilate, who was the Roman governor of Israel at that time, they were able to have Him put to death by crucifying him on a cross, outside the walls of Jerusalem. They didn't realise that in so doing they were fulfilling words of prophecy which had been written about Jesus hundreds of years before. Jesus came to earth specifically to die on a cross as a sacrifice for our sins, and to give us the free gift of eternal life. He knew that's how He would die, and He knew the religious leaders would be instrumental in it happening, but He still chose to come, even though He knew so many would reject Him. He knew He would be crushed, and have to suffer appalling agony, but He still came.

Those twigs were crushed and ruined, and the cross they made was destroyed. The cross Jesus died on is long gone, nothing remains, but it doesn't matter - it was only wood, and there was no power in it. What matters is that three days after the Son of God was crucified on the cross, God raised Him to life again, and He is alive for evermore. Unlike the crushed twigs that will never have life again, and are no use at all, Jesus is still alive, and for nearly 2,000 years since that happened He has been proving it by transforming literally billions of lives in amazing ways. I know it's true because He's done it for me, and He continues to do it every day of every year for people around the world.

Sadly, throughout the centuries since His death and resurrection, those same groups have existed. There have always been those who are angry with Him, those who hate Him, those who avoid Him, those who just can't seem to see who He is, and those who even today would love to put Him to death if He was on earth in bodily form. However, there are 2.3 billion people alive today who have chosen to follow Him because they know He's alive, and they've seen the truth of who He is, and what He does.

I wonder which group you're in? Let me ask you to look carefully at Jesus, and encourage you, if you're in any group other than the last one, to allow Him to show you how much He loves you, to allow Him to forgive you, and to bless and help you. He's available for you right now. You'll never regret it, so go on, why not give Him a try?

Swans

Driving down a country road one day, I saw, some way ahead at the bend, what appeared to be a swan about to walk along a track through some bushes. Before I reached the spot it was out of sight, but as I rounded the bend, there in front of me were two adult swans, and two cygnets, waddling slowly, and purposefully down the road. One adult was leading, the cygnets, which were about a third of the size of the parents, were in the middle, and the other adult was protecting the rear. They had crossed over from where they had been, and were walking down the left side of the road.

I drove slowly by, but it was such an unusual sight, and certainly something I'd never seen before, that a little further on I turned round, and drove back to see them again. As I came close, there was a car parked on my side, and the swans had almost reached it, so I stopped to let them pass. The ferocity of swans with young, when any potential threat gets too near, is well documented, but for some reason it didn't bother them to see me in the car, even though I was within just a few feet, and they walked slowly past. Once they had gone I drove on, turned round once more, went by again for the final time, and then continued on my journey.

It was such a pleasure to see them, but immediately I had real regret, because I didn't have my camera with me, and I would have been able to get some really good, and unique photo's. What made it worse was that only the previous day I had thought about taking it with me, but hadn't done it. The opportunity had gone, and it's very unlikely that I will ever see anything like it again. The trouble is, it's not the first time I've done that, and I've missed getting various unusual pictures, but I still don't learn. Once, when out with some friends, I had taken the camera with me, but decided to leave it in the car as I didn't think I would use it on the very short distance we were going to walk. As we walked towards some buildings, on top of the roof of one of them was a line of sparrows, and above them, perfectly positioned, was a beautiful rainbow. It would have made a great picture, but again the moment was lost, and all I can do is to keep thoughts of the scene in my memory.

Now, to miss taking some photo's is not exactly a life changing event, and other things we may regret having done, or not done, might not be either. I still think back at times to our wedding, and wish we had included some people on the guest list who we didn't invite, and wonder why we didn't invite them. It hasn't spoilt our marriage, or the relationship with the people, and it hasn't ruined my life, and yet I wish we'd asked them, but it can't be undone.

Other things can have a life changing effect though. Like us with the wedding guests, it may be a one off event, so it's not possible to start again, and do things differently. Whatever it was, we may have been damaged, or we may have damaged others, but it's there in the past, unchanging, and refusing to go away. The regret, the recriminations, and all sorts of other emotions linger on, continuing to cause damage.

However, like me with the camera, we can also keep doing the same thing wrong again and again. We may not want to do it, but we struggle with a particular problem time after time, feeling that we've failed once more. The regret is there, very probably coupled with the thought of, "if only I wasn't like this", or, "if only I didn't do this", or "if only, if only, if only", and it seems an unbreakable cycle. So many people think, "I can never change, there's no way out". There can be the regret of making the wrong career choice, looking back and wishing we'd done something else, but thinking it's too late now to change it. Added to that there can be the regret of being overlooked for promotion, with the long term hurt, resentment, or bitterness that can cause. The list of regrets can go on and on.

The problem with regrets is that they take away our joy, they bring us down, they spoil our lives, and relationships, and they can take away our hope for the future. Whether it's because of things we've done wrong, things people have done against us, or even perhaps because of missed opportunities which will never come again, no matter how much we wish they could, regrets stop us living life to the full, holding us firmly in the past. Whatever they are they can do us harm.

Apart from being beautiful to look at, I think it's wonderful that swans mate for life, that they care for each other, and that they are so protective of their young. I know they have far more power to do it than a lot of other birds and animals, but they will defend them at all costs. I once saw a swan by the side of a lake with two cygnets, smaller than those I had seen on the road. A totally irresponsible woman with a young Alsatian let it go very close to the swan, and didn't call it off, even though it was aggressive, but thankfully it was no match for the bird. The cygnets went into the water, but the parent was hissing, opening its wings, forcing the dog back without even touching it. Finally, when it was safe, the swan went into the water, and rejoined the cygnets. The adult swans I saw walking down the road were equally protective, one guarding the front and the other the rear. I don't know where they had come from, or where they were going, but the parents knew, and they were caring totally for their young.

That's what God is like with us. He knows where we've come from, He knows where we're going, He wants the best for us, and He cares for, and loves us totally. Just as the woman's lack of sense, and the aggression of the dog were overcome by the power of the swan, our faults and failures can be overcome by the power of God's love, but it's our choice. We can choose to keep God at bay, and continue carrying the regrets, the hurts, the resentments, the bitterness, or anything else which is bringing us harm, or we can come to Him, and accept His help. It may seem impossible, but He can free us from any of the things which are bringing us down and spoiling our lives. He even has the power to restore broken or damaged relationships, and change situations we thought could never be changed.

Although it was great to see the swans walking along in such an unusual setting, it looked as if it was hard work for them, as they are not really designed for a route march over tarmac. The elegance and grace they have on the water, and also in flight, were decidedly lacking, but they'd chosen the way they wanted to go, and had no alternative but to walk, because the cygnets were not yet able to fly. I can imagine them finally reaching a lake and walking straight in to bathe their aching feet, with the leading adult then saying, "Thank goodness that's over. Remind me not to do that again". The trouble is, the other adult would probably say, "That's what you said last time!" The difference with God is that He never gets it wrong.

As I've already said, we can make decisions which seem right at the time, but don't turn out that way, or we can actively decide to do something, knowing it's not the best thing to do. We can also make the same mistake over and over again, even when we don't want to. Quite simply, there are so many areas in life where we can get it wrong, no matter how hard we try not to, and we can carry regrets and bitterness with us to the grave, but we don't need to.

Jesus made it clear that we can ask God for forgiveness again and again, no matter how many times we fail, even if it's with the same problem, and that, when we really mean it, God will forgive us for that problem, or any problem, every time. Why? Because He can't stop loving us, He wants to help us leave the problems behind, whatever they are, and He wants to guide us in the right direction, so we can lead a life which is fulfilled, and worth living. He doesn't want us to waddle through life carrying those things, finding life hard going. He wants us to soar, and leave the regrets where they should be - forgiven, and in the past.

God is the God of new beginnings, who can wipe the slate clean, who can put us back on our feet, and give us everything we need to be the people He knows we can be.

The Christmas Tree

Driving into town one day in early January, I saw, lying on the pavement outside a house, a Christmas tree, which had obviously been put out for the dustmen. Gone were the decorations and lights which must previously have adorned it, and now, instead of the fresh green it would once have been, it was looking decidedly tired and dry. It had served its purpose, and so now had to be thrown out. The pleasure it brought was over, Christmas and New Year were gone, and so it was time to move on to the next thing to look forward to in the year, whatever that may have been for the people involved. It is something which is repeated for millions of people across the country every year.

Although I don't know what it meant for the owners of that tree, unfortunately, and sadly, for so many the real meaning of Christmas is lost in the tree, the presents, the parties, the television, and more. Just like the tree, Jesus, the real reason for the season, if He did manage to get a look in at all, is thrown out as soon as Christmas is over, to be left outside until Christmas comes again. For many, the only place Jesus will be at Christmas is at a carol service, where the nice cosy image of a baby surrounded by His parents, wise men, and animals, will bring them a warm or pleasant feeling for a short while, before they rush off to go through the final preparations for Christmas Day, leaving Him lying safely in the manger. For even more people, Jesus won't even get that far, and for them He's either totally irrelevant, or not even known about. I once heard a man in the street being interviewed on television, the reporter was asking him about Christmas, and he replied, "What has religion got to do with Christmas anyway?" Now, Christmas is solely about Jesus, the Christian faith is all about Him, but he had obviously either never heard, or never understood the reality of that.

A fairly recent phenomenon, has been the ever larger displays of lights inside and outside houses that are now necessary to show that you really do know how to play beat your neighbour out of doors. The competition is great, with some people starting to create their displays months before the day, and if an article about them appears in the local, or maybe even the national papers, they really have arrived. What Christmas is all about for them is portrayed everywhere.

There is Santa on the wall climbing up or down his illuminated ladder, next to an illuminated train and a flashing star, or on the roof he is sitting in his sleigh, or perhaps just standing there, surrounded by reindeer and snowmen, and hundreds of lights. On one side of the front door is a giant inflatable Santa, and on the other side an equally large snowman, both glowing brightly. Across the garden there are smaller versions of the same, mixed in with reindeer, whilst garlands of lights cover as much of the remaining space as possible. Everything cries out to those outside that this is the nearest thing they're going to find to the Blackpool illuminations. The cost of it all must have been colossal, and the electricity bill will soar, but isn't that what Christmas is all about? Surely the more lights there are the brighter life will be, and the happier Christmas will be too? Somehow though, it doesn't seem to work, in spite of all the effort involved in putting them up, and how much they cost.

Unfortunately, no matter how many lights there may be, they will never bring real light into people's hearts and souls, they can't bring the light and contentment people are looking for, and then, come January, the lights will go out again until next Christmas. Now, we have a Christmas tree, and decorations, and we give presents to those we love, although we do keep our spending within agreed, and very reasonable limits, but for us these things are optional extras, not what Christmas is all about.

Christmas really is only about Jesus. Without Him there wouldn't even be Christmas Day, and that alone shows the truth of who He is. That is why it is so sad that so many people are missing out on the reality of Christmas, and what the baby born in Bethlehem did for them, and what He can do for them. I think babies are wonderful, and I love to see them sleeping securely, or snuggling up to their mothers, innocent, and protected from harm. The problem is that no-one knows just what life has in store for a baby as it grows, and reaches adulthood, whether it will become a good or bad citizen, whether it will have a happy or sad life, and so much more.

Jesus, although He is the Son of God, and in spite of His great power, which He has had since before the creation of the world, was willing to leave the security of heaven, to come to earth and be born as a baby, in what was the scruffy and insignificant town of Bethlehem, as vulnerable and helpless as every new baby is. The difference is though, that, unlike human parents, God knew exactly what was going to happen to Jesus, where He would be born, what His life was for, and how and when He would die. That was His plan, and as I've said before, the birth, life and death of Jesus had been prophesied over many centuries. That plan was told by God to those prophets, and Jesus fulfilled it all.

For me, even when the tree goes, the reality of Christmas remains. The baby became a man, and, as a man, was crucified, hung on a cross to die an excruciating death, and in so doing He took the sins of the world upon Himself. The birth, death, and resurrection from death of Jesus Christ are the most significant events the world has ever seen. One of His titles is Prince of Peace. At Christmas and New Year there is so much talk and hope of there being peace around the world, but every year things just seem to get worse. The reason for that is that people are ignoring the Prince of Peace, and trying to fill their lives with anything but Him. Only Jesus can give every individual on this planet an inner peace that lasts all year, every year, if they are willing to receive it. The lights on the tree and Father Christmas go out, and stay out until next time. The light Jesus brings into the lives of everyone who asks Him to lasts all year, every year. Christmas is not about false hopes, temporary joy, and running away from reality for a short time. Christmas is the real thing, and the gift that Jesus offers us lasts forever.

Candle Smoke

One of my favourite smells is the one which comes from candle smoke just after the candle has been blown out, and the wick is still briefly smouldering. Now that may seem a strange thing to enjoy, but there is a particular reason why it gives me pleasure. Whenever it happens, that smell immediately takes me back to the happy childhood days at Christmas.

When I was a child we didn't have tiny lights on our tree. They weren't around, and instead we had small candles in holders clipped on various branches. For virtually the whole time the tree was there they weren't lit, as they would very quickly have burnt down and been a real danger, but on Christmas Day for just a short time we had them alight. My father would light them, or my brother and myself might be allowed to light some, but he would keep a watchful eye over them until he said they would have to be blown out, because it wasn't safe to leave them any longer. It was a shame when that happened, but we understood, and we'd had the excitement of having them alight for that brief time.

Children today would probably say that was pathetic, or whatever the current phrase may be, because they often have so much, and they want sophisticated things, but for us that time really was joyous. That is why, even today, the smell of candle smoke transports me straight back to the small front room of our council house, when my parents didn't have much money, and our presents weren't highly expensive, but they didn't bankrupt themselves either in getting them for us. A truly special time, when we were surrounded by their love, and Christmases were wonderful.

Sadly, today it seems that all that really counts is money. Retailers love Christmas for the boost to their turnover they hope to get, the shops start advertising their Christmas lines in August, credit card companies get ready to make a fortune, and the presents have to be bigger, and more expensive, every year. Although some of the big companies must hate Christmas Day because it means a whole day's sales have to be lost, for them there is always the great joy of opening on Boxing Day for the January sales, no matter how much harm it may do to the family life of their staff. For the shoppers there is the challenge of spending even more on Christmas presents than the previous year, and the delight of seeing just how big the credit card bill is when it arrives in January. One thing is certain, no lasting peace will be gained on either side of the counter, no matter how much has been spent.

Today, children want a DVD player, the latest computer, an Xbox, a mobile 'phone, and so much more. These days a lot of children get what they want, and sometimes even demand, and yet so many of them are bored, miserable, aggressive, and unhappy with their lives. As children there were things we asked for, but didn't always get, but the things we had gave us so much pleasure. It may have been a comic annual, a cowboy suit, a cap firing Winchester rifle, or various other toys over the years. The presents were never highly expensive, but it was always exciting unwrapping them, and they were always given with love.

These days there is no special feeling of Christmas. Everything in the build up to it is so often a rush, stress levels in people rise, there are family arguments, and so often people say they'll be glad when it's over. For many, as I said in the previous story, the reality of Christmas is irrelevant, and people are now far poorer in the quality of their lives because of it. When I was a child there was something special as Christmas approached, and Christmas Day really did feel different to any other day. I know it's possible to look back with rose coloured glasses, and imagine it was different when it wasn't, but I can honestly say that it truly was. My parents felt it too, because then Christmas wasn't just about money and more possessions. Christmas Day had a special feel that no other day in the year had.

Of all the decorations we had, one of my favourites was a small stable scene. It wasn't a full nativity set, just Jesus Christ in a manger, with Mary and Joseph with Him. It wasn't expensive, and yet for me it had to be out at Christmas. If you compared it with the tree, the decorations, and the presents, it was very small, and could have been regarded as being totally insignificant, and yet in that was a representation of the One who Christmas is all about, and that made it more important than all the other things put together.

You see, Jesus isn't still sleeping in a manger in Bethlehem, in some sort of time warp, which brings Him back once a year for a short time. He's alive now, today!

Without Him, it doesn't matter what people do to celebrate whatever it is they think they are celebrating, nothing about Christmas will make any lasting difference. It doesn't matter how much money is spent on presents which won't last, trying to buy happiness, it won't work, and probably after Christmas some things will have to go back for a refund anyway. It doesn't matter how many parties there may be, or whatever else people may do to celebrate, as any joy or peace will be temporary.

If you take Christ out of the word Christmas you are left with just three meaningless letters, 'mas', and what is there to celebrate in that? Yet that is what millions of people do every year. They all celebrate a Christ-less Christmas, but a Christ-less Christmas is meaningless, and there is no lasting joy in it. Jesus has to be in

Christmas for it to make sense, and for it to be something that's worth celebrating. Jesus is worth celebrating though, and not just at Christmas, but all year through, and He makes all the difference.

The smell of candle smoke takes me back to memories of very happy times, now far in the past. It's a very different world to the one I grew up in, and in many ways it's a much nastier world. More and more people have rejected God, and, as a consequence, violence, family breakdown, selfishness, greed, depression, alcoholism, drug dependency, depravity, and so much more have soared. Candle smoke can't actually take me back to wonderful childhood days, so that I can live them again, and not make the same mistakes I made growing to adulthood and beyond. Those days are gone forever, they can't be lived again, and I can't go back and stay safely in the past. I have to live in the present, and look to the future.

In spite of the thoughts the smoke brings, like life, the candles were potentially dangerous. In contrast, the stable scene represents total safety for us. I will remember the security, love, and joy of those childhood days for the rest of my life, but I'm so grateful that my past, my present, and my future are held safely in the hands of Jesus, and that the security, love and joy He gives will never end.

The Spider's Web

Have you ever watched a spider spinning a web? It's fascinating to see the way it steadily works round in a circle, with each section of silk added increasing the size of the web, until it's finally as big as the spider wants it to be. With numerous strands added all round, going across from the centre to the edge, they are amazing things to look at, and made with precision. Other lengths of silk are fixed to them, and are taken out to be anchors firmly attached to nearby objects or bushes. In spite of webs appearing to be so flimsy, they have surprising strength. They can hold the weight of numerous drops of water, and those anchor strands will keep them in place, even in strong winds. It's said that if the silk could be woven together to the thickness of a rope, it would be stronger than the rope.

Although we can find webs very attractive to look at, and may also marvel at how such tiny creatures can create something so intricate and precise in design, they are, in fact, deadly. Because the strands are so fine, many insects won't see them blocking the way to where they are flying, and although the way ahead might seem attractive, suddenly they are trapped. Held in the web's sticky silk there is no way out. I once saw a crane fly which was caught in a web, and was struggling to get out, but it was already too late. Immediately the spider had come out from where it was hiding, and injected it with poison. The crane fly kept moving, but it was getting much weaker, and the spider then started to wrap it in silk. In no time it was all over. The spider had successfully caught another victim.

So why have I talked about spider's webs? All through this book I've been explaining why Jesus came, and what He can do for us, but sadly, so many people don't see any need for Him, and reject or ignore Him. They may say they're okay, they've never robbed a bank, or murdered anyone, they've lived good enough lives for God to accept them, they're too busy, or a variety of other reasons. I've even had people say to me, and mean it, that they don't care if they do go to hell when they die. Believe me, that is frightening, because hell isn't a fun place. The reality is that it's a place of total evil, and there's permanent torment for those who have to go there.

The devil, or Satan as he is also known, is real. He's mentioned eighty eight times in the Bible, and Jesus talked about him, and He stood firm against him when the devil tried to tempt and trap Him. He's not a jokey little red character with horns and a trident, as we so often see him portrayed in cartoons. He's a force of unbelievable evil, and he's out to trap us, and destroy us.

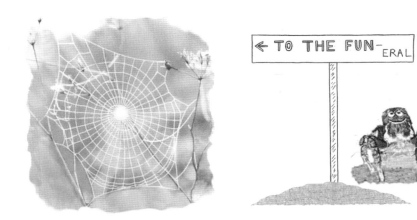

Just like the insects only seeing what looks like an attractive place to go to, but not seeing the snare that's there to catch them, we can be like that too. We may know what we would like to be doing, where we want to go, and how we hope, or intend our lives will be. When we are older, we may be looking back, seeing that because of what happened, life didn't work out the way we wanted it to. The trouble is, there are so many things around us every day which can tempt us, and take us off track, which can change, or even ruin our lives completely.

Spiders are experts at setting up traps to destroy their victims, and so is the devil. Unlike Jesus, who loves everyone in this world, and always has, and wants to give us all real life, the devil hates everyone, including those who follow him. He always has, and he wants to destroy everyone.

If we do see the traps the devil sets, they can seem very appealing, and very hard to resist, so much so that we may decide not to resist. Added to that, these days some people say there is no absolute right or wrong, and if it's right for you, then it's right. That is a complete lie, it's a trap of the devil, because God sets the standard, not us, and He says what is right and wrong. Deep down, we all really do know what is right or wrong, even if we try to push wrong things out of our thoughts to pretend they are okay. When we are tempted to walk into the trap, the devil will be saying things like, "Go on, it's what you want, it won't harm you, it will be fun, no-one will know, don't be old fashioned, everybody does it hese days".

It can be tempting to walk into the trap of adultery, or pornography. There may be the trap of stealing, whether from work in money or goods, from shops, or other people, or for those in business to deliberately overcharge, or cheat on taxes. It can be the trap of continuing to drink, even though it's destroying a person's health and relationships, or the trap of taking the first tablet to give a temporary high, which will lead down the road to hard drugs and death. It can be the trap of gambling, and all the harm that can cause. For all these, many people will probably say, "None of them apply to me, they're the really bad things, so I'm okay," but there are plenty of other traps for us. It may be lying, gossiping, being totally selfish, bitterness, anger, or getting pleasure in bringing people down with unkind and cruel words. The list goes on and on.

Other traps can be cleverly disguised, and we walk straight into them, because we don't even realise the very real danger that's there to catch us. Before I became a Christian I was dissatisfied with my life, and didn't know what to do to find the right way to go. Because of that I went to spiritualists, as they seemed to be able to know things they hadn't been told. On the surface it seemed to be okay, and supposedly they were just there to help, although it is clear they do like people to be generous with donations. What I didn't realise was, that in the Bible, God said very clearly that we shouldn't have anything to do with them. Why? Because they are not hearing from God, they are hearing from the devil.

They told me things which supposedly showed me the work I should be doing, and some other things about my life too. The trap was very cleverly laid, and what they said seemed very plausible, but thankfully I ignored their advice. Looking back later I realised that if I'd followed what they said, I would have been led into a life I didn't want, whereas God had something much better planned for me. He led me the right way into a life I did want. Also, if I had carried on with them, I know without doubt that I would have been trapped unwittingly into following the devil's ways, and kept totally away from God, and that would have been disastrous.

Ouija boards, tarot cards, horoscopes, and fortune tellers can appear to be able to help give direction, or perhaps just seem to be a bit of harmless fun, but they're not. Again, they are traps which open the way for darkness to come into people's lives, and keep them away from God, which is just what the devil wants. I will stop there, although that list could go on too, but remember, anything which keeps us from God is a trap.

That's why knowing Jesus, by allowing Him to come into our lives, is so important. It's about truth, freedom, peace, safety, real life. Whatever we may have done, whether it's any of those things I've listed, or anything else, Jesus is the only one who can forgive us, and set us free from them, so that one day, heaven is where we'll be headed. If I'd seen the crane fly before the spider came out, and had wanted to free it, I could have broken the web, but it was already too late. With Jesus, whatever web we may have been trapped in, no matter how strong it seems to be, He is able to break it completely, and free us totally, and it's never too late to ask Him to do that.

The Last Goodbye

When we were children, our parents took my brother and myself on holiday to stay on a farm in North Devon. The family who ran it were lovely people, the house was great, and so was the food, and we loved the area. We had a wonderful time, so much so that before we left my parents booked for the next year, and we eventually went there for six years in a row. The holidays there were always special, and we looked forward to going each year.

The problem was though that all too soon the holiday would come to an end, and it would be time to leave. Photos would be taken with us and their family, and there would be emotional goodbyes from us as we had to leave to go home. I remember one year in particular being quite upset that we had to leave, and my mother trying to console me with the fact that we would be going back to see my grandmother, who I loved very much, and that that was something to look forward to. Obviously, once we were home, life went back to normal, and the sorrow at leaving had gone.

However, many years later, I still hate saying goodbye when there is going to be a long parting from people I love. My brother and his family lived in Northern Ireland for 20 years, and it wasn't possible any more just to get in the car when we wanted to and drive half an hour to see them, the way it had been before they moved there. It meant we had to fly to Belfast, with all that entailed in booking flights beforehand, getting to the airport, having an hour's drive the other end to their home, and then later having to reverse the whole journey. It was no longer something we could do spontaneously, and frequently.

Whenever we were able to fly over, I would always experience that same anticipation of looking forward to being there with them that I'd had as a child for the holidays. My brother would be there for us at the airport, and there was the joy of meeting, and being together again. However, all too soon the time would come to an end, and he would take us back to the airport for the trip home. He would come into the terminal with us, and after checking in our luggage, it would be time to say goodbye before we went through the initial security check, leaving him on the other side of the barrier. As we walked away he would wait, and we would keep turning round to wave until we went out of sight. Just like the holidays, it was emotional and sad to be saying goodbye. Afterwards of course, we settled back into our usual routines, and were glad when the next opportunity to visit came.

Even though it was sad to be going home after our holidays, and it was sad to be leaving my brother and his family, there was always the thought that there would be another opportunity to do it again, even if it was some way in the future. However, the trouble with this life is that at some stage we are all going to come to that last goodbye, when it will be our time to leave this earth, and to leave everyone, and everything we know behind. There will be no turning back, no opportunity to do things we want to do again at some time in the future.

I don't know if you've ever driven into a place where for security they have spikes in the road which, if you're going the right way will go flat when you drive over them, but if you're going the wrong way, they will stay up, and if you continue they will stop you going through by puncturing your tyres. The last goodbye on this earth is final, and just as it is with the spikes, there's no way out. The good news is though, as I said in an earlier story, that this life isn't all there is.

When we go on any journey, there are always preparations to be made. If we're going on holiday we need to know where we're going, and how we're going to get there. Accommodation needs to be booked, we need to pack everything we need for the time we're away, and the list goes on. Even if we are only going somewhere on a bus ride we have to know the time it's coming, and we need to be sure we have the fare so we can travel on it. For any journey we need to be ready, and prepared.

I wrote just briefly in the story of Niagara Falls about our souls, but it's very important to understand the huge significance of them. We all of course have our physical bodies which we know are incredibly complex, but our bodies don't tell us what to do, we tell our bodies what to do. We have brains which are more powerful than any computer, which control our actions, but, unlike a computer with no emotions, built into us is something which guides our brains in the way we live. It directs us in every area of our lives, whether it's our emotions, the decisions we make every day, knowing what is right and wrong, how we relate to other people, and everything else that makes our lives what they are. It's who we really are. It's not the body we're living in during our temporary time on earth that does that. It's our soul which guides our life, the real us which can't be seen by a scan, but which we know is in us, controlling what we do, all through our lives. It's the part of us which doesn't die when our bodies do.

There are many, many people who've had well documented after death experiences, when their time for that final goodbye hadn't yet come. Some have died on operating tables, others have had heart attacks, and they've been resuscitated, and I've actually met a lady who died, and came back after her husband prayed for her. Some have had a belief in God, and others haven't, but all these people say they were travelling towards a bright light, and they had just a glimpse of what will happen at the final goodbye, when nothing can, or will bring them back. Sadly, we know our bodies have to die, and are finished, but it's our soul that doesn't die, and goes on to face God. The bodies of those people who've had after death experiences stayed where they were, but it was their soul which was going on.

The Bible too makes it very clear that this life isn't the end. I quoted the following verse in the chapter about the prize, but it's worth repeating, because it shows the reality of that fact. In John's Gospel, chapter 3, Jesus said, "For God so loved the world that He gave His one and only Son, that whoever believes in Him shall not perish, but have eternal life." He'd previously made it clear that it is our soul that can have eternal life. Also though, Jesus warned that we must be right with God to receive it. In Luke's Gospel, chapter 16, Jesus talked about a man who had rejected God in his life, and had ended up in hell, and just like the spikes stopping us on the road, He said there was no way to cross over from there to heaven. It was too late.

It says in the Bible that in heaven with God, there will be no more death, or mourning, or crying, or pain. There will in fact be no more parting, and no goodbyes. It is a place of incredible beauty, love, and peace which we will never have to leave. We need though to be prepared now, because if we leave it we may find the last goodbye comes before we're ready, and we've left it too late,

We can be guaranteed that wonderful future with God by praying the prayer at the end of this book, and then following Him in our lives. If we do that, the last goodbye will then take us into the first, and everlasting, 'hello.'

Closing Thoughts

Years ago we had blue tits nesting in a box on the wall of the house. They were the latest in a long line of occupants, and, as always, the parents worked frantically, swooping up the garden with insects for their young, then chasing off to get more. The chicks could be heard calling for their food, and everything was going well, but then suddenly it all went very wrong. For some reason the parents stopped coming. Whether they had been caught by a cat, or whether, very unlikely as it would have been, they had deserted the nest, we didn't know.

The hours passed with no sightings, and although we made 'phone calls to see if there was anything we could do to help the babies, the advice we were given was that there was really nothing at all. We didn't have the skills and speed to catch insects, and find grubs in trees to give them the food they needed, and we just had to wait. Gradually the chirping stopped, eventually we knew they were dead, and I had the very sad job of removing the perfectly formed bodies of those beautiful little birds from the nest. That box, which had been a place of new life, had become a place of death, and we had no power to do anything about it.

In contrast, as I've said before, God has the power to help us in every situation, because He is the absolute expert in everything. This planet is where we first began life, and it is where our lives will end, but we have a God who can provide everything we need during our lives, both physical and spiritual. He will never desert us, for He said that when we trust our lives to Him He will never leave us or forsake us. He is the one who sent Jesus to die on the cross for our sins so that our death isn't the end, but the beginning. Jesus is the One who said about those who follow Him, "I give them eternal life, and they shall never perish; no-one can snatch them out of My hand," (John chapter 10, v. 28). We can trust God never to abandon us, and never to reject us.

Another year, in the same box, different parents raised their brood successfully, and early one fine morning the chicks were ready to leave. One by one they came to the hole, leaning further and further out, until suddenly, encouraged by their parent's calls, they took their first flight to the freedom of their new lives outside the box.

Finally, there was just one chick left. It would get to the hole, look out, and then drop back down, only to repeat the process shortly afterwards. This happened a number of times, and once, it was half way out. It seemed it must fly, but somehow it didn't have the courage to do it. An inch further and it would have had no option but to go, and to start living the life it was meant to live. We were longing to see it fly, but, after hesitating, it didn't do it, and went back in the box. The problem was that each attempt to leave took energy, and it wasn't long before it became obvious that those attempts were becoming feebler, and less frequent.

The parents too had a problem. They were now very busy looking after their lively youngsters, who were happily flying around in the trees, but were taking up more of their time. The visits to the box with food became less frequent, so the baby grew weaker. Eventually the parents stopped coming, there was no sound from the chick, and the end was inevitable. It was very hard to watch, but no amount of encouraging by the parents had been able to persuade the baby to make that first flight. It had turned away from freedom and new life, and paid the price. The parents had no option but to let it go.

Sadly, many people are like that with God. He offers them freedom, wholeness, and a life worth living, but they choose to reject Him, and not accept the free gift of life. If people decide they don't want God in their lives, when they come to the end and have to face Him, it's too late. They have left Him with no option but to let them go into an awful eternity without Him, whilst He is with those eternally who chose to receive new life through Jesus Christ.

Some would like to experience God in their lives, but they just can't seem to take that final step, and instead hold back. It can seem very scary stepping out of what we know, but God can be trusted totally. Whether people choose to reject God, or whether they miss out on Him by a mile, or, like the bird, an inch, the end result is the same.

My desire in writing this book is that you will come to know Jesus Christ as your Lord and Saviour, and find every good thing I've described that He offers us all. Let me encourage you to take that step, and not to miss out on knowing the love of God, not even by an inch.

If you are now ready to do that, and to receive Jesus into your life, all you have to do is to pray and mean a simple prayer. The way to pray is to be honest with Him about your situation, ask Him for forgiveness, and invite Him into your life, then He will do the rest. When you talk to Him like that, you're praying, it's between you and Jesus, and that's all you need.

Now it may be that you've never prayed in your life before, and don't know where to begin, and you may believe in God and Jesus, or you may not. Because of that, there is a prayer written for you below if you do believe, which you can repeat, and one for you if you don't believe, or have doubts. If you pray either of these prayers and mean them, I know Jesus can, and will come, even if you consider yourself to be an atheist, and He will show you that He's real.

The prayers:

"Lord Jesus, I know that I have done many things wrong in my life, and I am truly sorry for them all. I ask you to forgive me now for everything I have ever done wrong, and to wash me clean. I believe you are the Son of God, and that you died on the cross for my sins. I ask you to come into my life now, and be my Lord and Saviour now, and for eternity. Thank you for dying for me, and I accept you as my Lord and Saviour now, and ask you to help me to follow you always. Amen."

or:

"I know that I have done many things wrong in my life, and I truly am sorry for them all. You know my doubts, but Jesus, if you really are the Son of God, and You died for my sins, I want to know you. I ask you to forgive me now for everything I have ever done wrong, and to wash me clean. I ask you to come into my life now, to show me your love, and the truth of who You are, and be my Lord and Saviour, now and for eternity, and I accept you into my life now. Amen."

If you have been able to pray either prayer, or one of your own along similar lines, and meant it, Jesus now lives in you, He has forgiven you for everything you have ever done wrong, and has washed the past clean. What He will do for you I don't know, because your needs are unique to you, but He knows everything about them, and He will do what is best for you when you let Him. Just relax, and receive His peace into your life, let Him give you hope for the future, and show you the way forward. You can pray to God as often you want to, at any time, day or night, for whatever your needs are.

It means you are now a Christian, and it will be beneficial for you to meet with other Christians, because they will be able to help you grow in your new found faith. You will find them in churches where the minister obviously has a real and living faith in Jesus, which shows through in the sermons, and in the lives of the people in the church. Unfortunately, there are churches where it's more about boring religion and rituals, and where there is very little about Jesus, so avoid them, as they'll do you no good at all. Christianity involves receiving love and help from God, but also receiving love and help from the people who have a real faith, and are clearly following Him, so don't be afraid to meet them.

Also, it will be really beneficial to start reading the Bible (use a modern translation), and although at first it may seem hard to understand, the more you read it the easier it becomes. It will show you so much about the love and power of God and Jesus. There is a lot to learn about God, and His love for you, but don't be put off by the thought of that - it is a gradual process which will go on for the rest of your life, and there is no exam, no test at the end of it. Just like our lives, there is always more to discover. We can never find out all there is to know about God, but the more we learn of Him, the closer we can get to Him. When you let Him, He will start to make changes in your life, but don't worry about that either. Some may be gradual, almost imperceptible, whilst others may be quicker, but whatever they are they will be for your benefit, because God only wants the best for you, and He wants to bless you. If He was willing to send His Son to die for you, He certainly won't do things to harm you. There is nothing to fear, but it is good to have experienced Christians around you to explain things which at this stage you may not understand.

Finally, let me assure you that you can trust Jesus in every situation. Jesus died for you, He has chosen you, He has called you by name, He loves you, He will help and guide you, and He will never let you go. Just follow Him, and He will show you the best way forward for your life.

If you would ike more information or help please write to
johnchapter3v.16@protonmail.com

Modern translations of the Bible include The Good News Bible, The New International Version, The New King James Version, The New Living Translation.